A Note on the Author

JOHN DEERING was born in Fulham in 1967. He has lived in Middlesex, Oxfordshire, Essex, Surrey, Toulouse and Edinburgh. He is the author of *Team on the Run: The Inside Story of the Linda McCartney Cycling Team* and *12 Months in the Saddle,* and is a regular contributor to *Ride Cycling Review.* He lives in Richmond-upon-Thames with his Giant Defy Advanced.

Bradley Wiggins:
Tour de Force

JOHN DEERING

This edition first published in Great Britain in
2013 by Arena Sport an imprint of

Birlinn Ltd
West Newington House
10 Newington Road
Edinburgh
EH9 1QS

www.birlinn.co.uk

ISBN 978 1 78027 129 3
eBook ISBN 978 0 85790 532 1

British Library Cataloguing-in-Publication Data
A catalogue record for this book is available
on request from the British Library.

Typeset by Hewer Text UK Ltd, Edinburgh
Printed and bound by Clays Ltd, St Ives plc

This book is for Brad.
For always being Brad.

Contents

PROLOGUE:

Liège

Saturday, 30 June 2012

It's approaching seven minutes past five on Saturday, 30 June 2012. The 188th rider to begin this year's Tour de France is inhaling deeply in the small start house that will fire him on his way towards Paris. There may be 3,500km to go, 90 hours of saddle time, the Alps, the Pyrenees, a defending champion to conquer and he may have finished no higher than fourth in this race before *and* only ever finished it three times, but that doesn't alter the fact that the 188th starter is the favourite to win. He's British, too. His name is Bradley Marc Wiggins OBE.

We're in Liège. Not France – Belgium. The Tour de France makes regular sorties beyond its natural borders (notably for the start), usually every two years or so. In 2007, Bradley stood in a similar Tour de France start house waiting for his moment to begin, but in his home city of London. As the reigning World and Olympic Pursuit Champion, the short-time trial format of the prologue made him a big favourite to take the first yellow jersey of the race and Brad's first stage win in the Tour de France. On that day, home expectation got the better of him and he was beaten into fourth place by one of his opponents today, Switzerland's Fabian Cancellara. But that was 2007, when Brad's sole aim was that short sprint around the streets of Westminster. Today he has bigger fish to fry. He wants to win the Tour de France.

Behind the mirrored mask of his aero helmet visor, Brad closes his eyes and visualises the course in front of him, the corners and the bends. He knows that the Tour de France lasts three weeks and can't be won on any one day, but it can be lost in the blink of an eye. Last year he found himself in a ditch with a broken collarbone after a week's racing. His predecessor as World and Olympic Pursuit Champion and British Tour hope, Chris Boardman, hadn't even made it through the 1995 prologue when a horrific crash in storm-battered Brittany ruled him out with a shattered ankle after just a few minutes of the prescribed three weeks.

It would be nice to win today, but far from essential. Laying down a marker to his rivals before the race has begun in earnest would be a good thing, but would also raise a separate conundrum: will Brad's Team Sky want to defend the yellow jersey that he will wear as winner of the prologue for twenty more stages? Especially as they are here with the stated second objective of helping his teammate, World Champion Mark Cavendish, to win as many stages as possible. The number one priority is to get around safely without losing any time to his most significant rivals: Cadel Evans, Vincenzo Nibali, Jurgen Van Den Broeck, Denis Menchov. There is a queue of suitors for the final yellow jersey in Paris.

It's a fine day, with no showers, high winds or thunderstorms to worry about. French time trial champion Sylvain Chavanel has held the best time since earlier this afternoon. The first serious challenger to his position is the TT specialist Tony Martin of Germany. Wearing a white skinsuit emblazoned with the rainbow bands that tell everybody he is indeed the champion of the world in this discipline, Martin certainly looks the part and sets a furious tempo around the boulevards alongside the river Meuse. Misfortune awaits him though, and his low-profile carbon time trial bike has to be replaced just after the halfway point in the 6.4km race when he picks up a puncture. He gets a superfast bike change from his Omega mechanic in the following car, but you can't change bikes and win prologues when they're this short. The World Champion will end up sixteen seconds behind Chavanel, near enough to feel that he could have won if his luck had been in.

Jurgen Van Den Broeck, a true threat in the mountains to come, although not one in short bursts against the clock as today, rolls down the start ramp and takes to the road. It's time for Bradley to step up. Breathing deeply and smoothly, intent on the road ahead, his red sideburns peeking out from below the billiard ball Team Sky aero helmet, he knows that the waiting is over at last. Every day since last year's heartbreaking crash on the road to Châteauroux, Brad has been dreaming of this day, the chance to put it all right. All the training, all the racing, all the famous victories he has already strung together this season point to today in Liège. The starter raises his hand to count off the seconds. A few more deep breaths and Brad sets his jaw. Time to stand up and be counted. He's off.

The route heads along the Meuse, often doubling back on itself to head down the opposing carriageway. Though an all-out effort is required for a shot at victory, control and caution are needed at the corners, often full 180-degree turnabouts. Brad's awareness of his power output and what he needs to deliver to win is acute, but he also knows that his Pinarello time trial machine is a weapon built for speed in straight lines, not for zipping around city streets. He blasts along the wide boulevards but slows carefully for the tight angles, warned continuously by the calm voice in his ear, his *directeur sportif* (DS) Sean Yates in the car behind. Together they have been over this course many times in the past few days of preparation.

Brad is in tenth place at the first time check. Has he kept something under the bonnet? It appears that he has. The long sweeping roads of the second half of this short race see the Brit begin to open the throttle. His long illustrious history in track pursuiting has left him with an almost preternatural ability to time and judge his effort. World Junior Champion at just seventeen years of age and later World Champion at the same event no fewer than three times, Brad knows how to keep his effort steady and increase the pace relentlessly as he closes on the line.

He plunges down the boulevard d'Avroy and breaks the beam on the finish line fractions of a second quicker than the long-time leader Chavanel who smiles ruefully at his luck. It's now Brad's turn to wait. Just about to leave the start house a short distance away is Mr Prologue himself, Fabian Cancellara. The Swiss has brought home the prologue bacon no fewer than four times in the Tour de France, the first time being in this very city in 2004 when he consigned Lance Armstrong in his pomp to a shock defeat. The rumours among the press band in Liège were that Spartacus was on the way out, his legs not what they were, his collarbone still uncomfortable since his heavy crash in the Tour of Flanders in April, and younger riders were ready to grab his crown.

Perhaps they were a little hasty. Cancellara, despite the top ten riders home being separated by a mere handful of seconds, astonishingly thumps seven seconds into Wiggins in second. Tour de France prologue number five is his, and so is that coveted first yellow jersey.

Bradley Wiggins is quietly satisfied. He has taken a little time from every one of his rivals for the overall victory and saved his team from the effort of a fraught first week protecting the yellow jersey. He hasn't won the battle, but in the first skirmish in the war of the Tour de France 2012, he has put fear into the hearts of his enemies.

'I'm really calm, really relaxed. I keep taking myself back to reality by putting my headphones on and just taking myself out of this madness, because this isn't reality at the moment. It'd be very easy to get drawn into all this,' says Brad after his iPod-soundtracked warmdown on the rollers as he attempts to brush off the chaos that is always attendant around team buses at the Tour. 'Bit of Otis Redding.'

Liège–Seraing, 198km

Sunday, 1 July 2012

Sky like to do things differently.

Dave Brailsford transformed British track cycling through using professional training methods and preparation, and leaving nothing to chance. His GB national set-up reached its zenith at the 2012 Olympics when they grabbed seven of the ten gold medals on offer.

Brailsford had long dreamed of transferring the success of the track squad to the road. He knew as well as anybody that success in the velodrome meant Olympic success and huge national pride, but in cycling it's the road that matters. In 2007 he began to talk openly about establishing a pro road set-up, somewhere that the track prodigies coming through the national system could aim their sights. Riders like Bradley Wiggins, Mark Cavendish and Geraint Thomas had all been key members of the track performance programme, but all of their ultimate goals lay on the tarmac of Europe. What if Brailsford could build an umbrella organisation to keep these talents together? It would have to be a British team with a British sponsor, a national team for the country to unite behind in a way that had never happened in cycling before.

The 2007 Tour de France, after the amazing weekend in London that kicked it off, developed into one of the most exciting contests in the long history of the race. A stick-thin pale Danish boy called Michael Rasmussen and a prodigiously talented Spanish rider by the name of Alberto Contador knocked seven bells out of each other every time the course headed uphill. It was riveting viewing, and many man-hours were lost as bike fans the world over bunked off work to follow the daily drama. The battle royal raged across France with the combatants drawing on superhuman exertion to put one over each other.

But Rasmussen's efforts were indeed superhuman. His challenge unravelled as a trail of missed drugs tests and a sorry story of 'vampire' dodging, during which he led the UCI testers a merry dance as they attempted to pin him down, saw him thrown off the race. The reputation of the Tour and the sport itself was once again swimming in detritus at the bottom of the world's dirtiest sink. In fact, make that the world's least appealing urinal, as double stage winner Alexandre Vinokourov went out the same exit door of shame after brazenly cheating the blood doping regulations.

With the French press gloomily announcing 'le mort du Tour' and the legacy of dozens of sordid tales of doping, cheating, lying and subterfuge littering the sport's recent history, this was one of cycling's lowest moments. It certainly felt that way to those fans who had been avoiding the morning commute to cheer on their heroes. Heroes with feet of clay, it now seemed. Even Bradley Wiggins, a frequent and outspoken critic of doping, found himself drawn into the 2007 mess when his teammate on the French Cofidis squad, Cristian Moreni, tested positive for testosterone. The hormone is known as 'the idiot's drug' in cycling due to the strong chance of you being caught if you abuse it. The whole team were removed from the race, showing that even the most vehement of protesters can find himself tarred with a great big dirty brush.

How would Dave Brailsford be able to put his master plan into action against this tawdry backdrop? He faced the issue head on, talking about providing an antidote to the constant negative stories – 'the doom and gloom' as he called it. The garlanded cycling writer Richard Moore would even later mischievously suggest that Brailsford was perhaps using 'the logic of the property market: buy when prices are low'.

As it happened, in the end, the deal almost came to Brailsford rather than him chasing down the cash in the traditional way of these things. Sky, the Murdoch empire's broadcasting giant, were looking for a sport in which to get involved – a sport they could own publicity-wise, a sport that worked on a myriad of different levels from children's participation through family leisure pursuits via fitness fanatics to the best professional outfit in the game. Sponsors have a closer relationship with their teams in cycling than any other sport. Steven Gerrard doesn't play for Carlsberg, he plays for Liverpool. Lewis Hamilton doesn't drive for Santander, he drives for McLaren. But Bradley Wiggins and Mark Cavendish, in 2012 at least, ride for Sky. There's value in that.

In fact, even more value than you might think. Sky, under the aegis of BSkyB, the operating company, directly paid £6m towards the running of the team in 2011, the last year for which figures are available at the time of writing. This came out of the company's marketing budget, which was, for the same period, wait for it, £1.2bn. OK, we don't know the costs for 2012, and expensive arrivals like Mark Cavendish don't come cheap, however, the transfer costs incurred by the team when buying Wiggins, among others, out of his previous contract, will have disappeared. So, let's just suppose for a minute that BSkyB put in the same amount of money in 2012 as they did in 2011. That means the entire publicity attained by the team in this glory-soaked season accounts for just 0.5% of their total marketing spend. That sounds like the sort of value most people can appreciate.

It sounded very much like a match made in heaven.

★

In the spirit of doing things differently, Sky had given themselves what Brailsford would call a 'nice problem to have'. When the team was eventually launched at the beginning of the 2010 season, he talked confidently of producing a 'British winner of the Tour de France within five years'. Gasps of amazement, even ridicule, were heard around the cycling world, but they were scared of Sky's power. Ever since 2010, it had been clear that the man chosen to fill those intimidating shoes of destiny was Bradley Wiggins. Team Sky arrived in Liège on the last weekend in June 2012 with the avowed aim of delivering victory for Wiggins in Paris.

The 'nice problem to have' was Mark Cavendish. In the interests of building their British team and thus hiring the best British riders, they had spent years courting the fastest finisher in the sport, possibly the fastest ever finisher in the sport. The Manx rider came at a high price, but he also arrived as the World Champion, BBC Sports Personality of the Year and the winner of twenty stages of the Tour de France. The question was: could Team Sky deliver on both fronts? Could they guide Wiggins to overall victory and simultaneously lead Cavendish to the stage wins they had signed him for? Could they support Cav's bid to win the points jersey while Wiggins fought for the biggest prize? Wiggo in yellow and Cav in green?

There was a precedent. In 1996, the German T-Mobile team had managed to win the race with Bjarne Riis, take second place with the emerging Jan Ullrich and the green points jersey for the speedy Erik Zabel. Zabel had become a confidant of Cavendish in recent years, guiding the young Brit when he first entered the world of Tour de France sprinting at that same T-Mobile set-up. However, things had been different for Cavendish at the various incarnations of the High Road/HTC/Columbia team from which he arrived at Team Sky. There, he was king of the castle. Da man. They surrounded him with powerful *domestiques* like Bernie Eisel and race-proven sprinters in themselves like Matt Goss and Mark Renshaw whose sole purpose was to get the Manx Missile to the finish line in the right place to do his thang. And his thang invariably involved a big grin and a victory salute. How would they cope with those demands and the need to control the race for Brad? Would they be able to sit on the front all day to dissuade attacks, chase down escapees, keep Wiggins out of the wind, line out the bunch in the high mountains, protect a potential yellow jersey for many days on end *and* produce a high-speed train to lead out Cavendish? It was a tall order. Perhaps Cav would revert to his early-career style of joining the trains of other sprinters' teams as they pounded towards the line in tight formation before popping round them cheekily to take the victory for himself? A young prodigy might get away with that for a season in his youth, but the World Champion at the world's biggest team would make himself few friends. And you need friends in bike racing or bad things start to happen.

Stage 1, from Liège to Seraing, would help us find out.

★

Fabian Cancellara looks good in yellow. Five prologue wins have delivered him plenty of days in the *maillot jaune* over the years, and his power on the hard roads and fast stages of the Tour's first week have often kept him in the front of the race until it meets the mountains. The Swiss hero loves racing in Belgium and northern France, too, as his dominating victories in the Tour of Flanders and Paris–Roubaix have proved. His grin tops the yellow jersey with pride as the Tour rolls out *en masse* for the first time.

Bike racing has changed considerably in the last few years. In the old days, races would be packed with lengthy stages that would begin at a leisurely pace before rocketing through the final hour at a furious speed as the sprinters' teams vied for supremacy in the final shakedown. These days, bizarrely, the fastest hour is often the first. This is because, with stage wins at such a premium, everybody is keen to get in 'the break'. Not *a* break, but *the* break. The second the commissaire's flag is withdrawn inside the red car at the front to signify that neutralisation is over and racing can begin, riders begin firing themselves out of the bunch and haring off up the road. The peloton, filled as it is with other riders who want to be in the break, quickly accelerates to breakneck speeds to bring them back. There are plenty of riders here who have no hope of winning the overall prize and no hope of winning sprint stages, who will lose out in the time trials and get destroyed in the mountains. What they crave is the chance of a stage victory, getting themselves into a tasty little move, outrunning the bunch and outfoxing their breakaway companions to taste Tour glory. They will also be doing their hard-pressed teammates a favour, as they can relax in the bosom of the bunch, safe in the knowledge that their buddy up the road will save them from a day killing themselves at the front to bring it all back.

Liège on Stage 1 is no different to this pattern, and Cancellara's RadioShack-Nissan team ride tempo while various hopefuls launch themselves towards Seraing. Those trying to digest their generous breakfasts in the crowd behind are delighted when things calm down a little sooner than is often the case and the break forms. Six riders, no famous names, no danger to those with their eye on ultimate glory. After a few moments of jousting with the sextet a handful of yards in front of them, the peloton relents and they gather themselves for a few minutes, Cancellara's men ensuring it doesn't get silly and jeopardise his yellow jersey.

This morning in the Team Sky bus, Sean Yates had laid out the day's priorities:

No crashes.
Keep Brad safe.
Put a rider in the break.
Keep the race together in the final stages for Cav.
Lead out Cav.
Give Edvald Boasson Hagen free rein.

The first week of the Tour de France is a dangerous place to be. People fall off. Dreams are shattered. The best laid plans of mice and bike riders et cetera. When Wiggins hit the deck, resplendent in his newly acquired GB Champion's jersey twelve months ago, it was the death of a million hopes for British bike fans, not to mention the man himself, his team and his family. Crashes happen, but there are things that can be done. It's safer to ride near the front. It's better to have your teammates around. And it's good if it's not raining.

If there's a rider from Team Sky in the break, less work is required from his teammates to chase things down. It's also an opportunity to win a stage if the move stays clear, or even a chance to take yellow when time gaps are so narrow at this early stage in the overall competition.

Cav's requirements become more accentuated the nearer we get to the finish. If he's in there, he's trusted to win. He's the fastest man here out of the 200-odd riders competing. If the team can bring him through, they will.

Edvald Boasson Hagen, champion of Norway, is a popular man at Team Sky. Blessed with immense strength, he has the ability to blast his way to victory on hard days. His overall hopes are hampered by his difficulties in the high mountains, but he is a wild card, a quality accessory that any team would be glad to have. Let him go his own way.

The crashes have begun. First to hit the deck is Tony Martin, his run of bad luck continuing after a puncture robbed him of a big shout in yesterday's prologue. He carries on with a battered wrist, lacerated elbow and sour demeanour.

Team Sky regroup around their leader and settle in for the long haul, taking it in turns to make sorties back to Yates's car and return with bottles. It's a showery day, and as the pace picks up towards the day's *dénouement*, things become increasingly fraught. The six escapees show no desire to be caught, and though the RadioShack-Nissan-powered peloton closes the gap to a minute with 30km left to ride, they grit their teeth and press on gamely.

The dreaded shout of '*Chute dans le peloton!*' crackles Yates's radio, and he cranes his neck round the cars and riders in front to see who has gone down. Luis Leon Sanchez from Rabobank is hurt . . . a couple of Spanish guys . . . oh shit, a

Team Sky jersey. It's his trusted road captain, Australia's Mick Rogers. Vastly experienced and a former contender himself, Rogers is Yates's eyes and ears in the bunch. He is bumped and bruised but uninjured. Yates lets out a breath he has been holding for some time and chases after the race, now closing inexorably on the six men in front and the finish in Seraing.

Cavendish moves up under the patronage of his minder Bernie Eisel. Eisel arrived at Team Sky from HTC with Cavendish and has been at his side unstintingly for the last couple of years.

The big danger to the pure sprinters – Cavendish, Greipel, Farrar, Petacchi – is the siting of a nasty little hill within the finishing town of Seraing. It's clear that several riders have this in mind, and the pace reaches crazy levels as the escapees are finally gobbled up and those with aspirations push on. There is a huge roar from the crowds beneath the finish line's big screens as the yellow jersey himself, Spartacus, Fabian Cancellara launches a searing move with just 1,500m to go. He tears the field apart with the burst, but two men just manage to hang on to him: powerful Slovak Peter Sagan and our own Edvald Boasson Hagen. Unable to rest lest they be reeled in by the desperate bunch, Cancellara opens the sprint, but he's easily overhauled by a blistering burst from Sagan who has time to pull off a dancing victory salute as he crosses the line. Edvald is third. A powerful performance but not at the level of Sagan. Cancellara has lost the stage but retained the jersey and his famous grin.

What of Cavendish? Like the other pure sprinters, the speed and the severity of the final short climb was too much for him to be in a position to compete and he saved his finish for the following day, rolling in among the main field in 128th place.

Wiggins, however, has had a first stage to remember. Having avoided the mishaps that have split the bunch at times, including the spill that put his captain Mick Rogers on the deck alongside him, Bradley has stayed calm, maintained his position in the bunch and, despite not having designs on stage victory, positively flew up the last climb to take an excellent sixteenth spot on the stage alongside his main rivals Evans and Nibali. He will look them in the eye tonight and say, 'I'm coming for you.'

⦿

PEOPLE ALWAYS WANT TO talk about Bradley's dad, but it's his mum they should be talking about.

Linda was a seventeen-year-old local girl with a love of bike racing when she met Garry Wiggins near her home in West London. She was a regular at the local track and her pretty blonde looks and independent nature soon brought her to the attention of the attractively cavalier Australian rider who was one of the more impressive guys to be seen on the Paddington track. He hit on her, she hit on him back and she found herself with a rather exciting and rakish boyfriend five years her senior.

Garry had arrived from provincial Victoria with a bike, a few Aussie dollars, and a burning ambition to make a name for himself in European cycling. He bullied his way on to what was then a thriving track scene, using his skill, his power and his fists when necessary.

In 1979, Linda married Garry and they decided to set up home in Belgium to further Garry's racing career. His plans lay not on the road but on the lucrative six-day circuit. The six-day is a popular niche event in some areas today, but it was big news in the 1970s and 1980s. A circus of riders would move from town to town and set up shop in an arena for a week where they would ride either on the boards of a permanent track or one constructed for the occasion. There was an annual event at Wembley Arena, or Empire Pool as it was then known, called the Skol Six. The gloriously named event brings back images of cheap beer sloshing around in plastic glasses and men hurling encouragement and abuse at sportsmen while scarcely noticing what is going on. A bit like Saturday afternoon in the Tavern at the Lord's Test.

The riders would perform in pairs over six nights of racing, riding a form of tag-team racing called the madison after Madison Square Garden in New York, where the discipline had developed. Effectively, only one of the pair is racing. The other tends to roll around the top of the banking out of the way. When his teammate is flagging, he hurls his fresher partner into the action with a handsling. One of cycling's more dangerous stunts, the handsling, along with the harem-scarem nature of the random tags going on at any moment, makes the madison extremely exciting to watch, but hard to follow. Hence the booze and the hollering hordes.

Garry Wiggins was pretty good at it. From the Wiggins's little apartment in Ghent he would race most days in the summer, competing in the small circuit races known as *kermesses* that each small town staged on its local roads. Then in the winter it would be on to the tracks of the six-day ring in Belgium, Holland, Germany and Switzerland, and a chance to earn some proper money.

It was into this strange world that Bradley Marc Wiggins arrived on 28 April 1980. Unlike anything that happens at Team Sky these days, in 1980, Bradley was very much Not Part Of The Plan. Garry had already managed to leave one family behind in his life – a wife and daughter from a teenage marriage in Australia – and now the second one was coming under some pressure. Amphetamine use was rife in those long days and nights of sustained racing and the lack of proper doping controls meant that riders were often looking for the other type of speed to get them through their working weeks. Garry filled that need for himself and plenty of others by being the go-to man in Ghent if you needed a helping hand with what cyclists have always euphemistically termed medication. According to Brad himself, writing in his excellent 2009 autobiography *In Pursuit of Glory,* after a family visit to Australia, Garry smuggled back a whole bunch of amphetamines in his baby's nappy. That must make Brad the youngest drug offender on the cycling circuit by some distance.

Amphetamines, booze, a hard man's nature and a temper. It must have been pretty tough for Linda, struggling to look after a baby at her young age in a small apartment in a foreign country. People are often mistaken that being in Belgium, a dual-language country, means that people speak both French and Flemish. In fact, it's much more like England and Wales: you wouldn't expect to walk into a supermarket in Norwich and be understood if you asked for your lottery ticket and 20 Marlboro Lights in Welsh. That's Belgium. Wallonia in the south is pure French; Flanders in the north is all guttural Flemish, a language that has been described as sounding like a rural version of Dutch. Linda's French lessons from school weren't very useful for integrating into Ghent society. A drunken, angry and sometimes violent husband was the last thing she and her baby needed.

The couple struggled through to Christmas 1982, fighting, breaking up and reuniting regularly, until Garry didn't turn up in England as planned for a family Christmas. He'd decided to spend it with his new girlfriend instead. That was it as far as his attempt at happy families went.

A child's bike turned up on Brad's third birthday, but that was the only thing he or Linda got out of the itinerant elder Wiggins for the rest of the boy's childhood. And Linda certainly didn't miss the black eyes.

Linda's parents, George and Maureen, were a godsend. While she worked around the clock to provide for her young boy, his grandparents did all they possibly could to help and support her. She moved back home – even though her two sisters were still there – and the family dug in and helped each other out. It wasn't long before the hard-working young mum had grafted her way into a proper flat for herself and her toddler, within walking distance of the old place in Paddington.

Granddad George was Bradley's constant companion in those early days. Sport ran through George like working-class blood, but the sports he took Brad to week in, week out during those formative years were far removed from the Tour de France. For racing and excitement, it wasn't the velodrome, it was the greyhound tracks of London; and for guile and craft it was snooker and darts in the British Legion.

Linda unsurprisingly found herself a new man, despite not having much time for looking with her long hours and her inquisitive schoolboy running around her skirts at every other moment. Brendan was a thoroughly decent guy who respected and nurtured Bradley through his school years, and he and Brad's mother also gave the boy a brother, too, Ryan, seven years Brad's junior.

Bradley Wiggins was a typically bright London schoolboy, popular enough at school, well loved at home, playing football in the streets and parks with his mates, getting in and out of the odd scrape but nothing to write home about. Where was the genesis of the Tour de France hero? How did this gangly smiling kid become a World Champion and Olympic gold medallist?

Visé–Tournai, 207.5km
Monday, 2 July 2012

Each team in the Tour de France is made up of nine riders. The designated leader of the team wears a number ending in one, hence Bradley Wiggins's 101. Each of the riders has a specific role. Team Sky is as follows:

101: Bradley Wiggins. The leader. The man. The one. The reason we're all here. Fourth in this race three years ago, he revealed his potential. His first Tour with Team Sky was also Team Sky's first Tour and it proved to be a steep learning curve for both parties. In 2011 he arrived in great form with an improved team but was an early crash victim. This year he starts as the favourite to win the race.

102: Edvald Boasson Hagen. The wild card. A massive talent, champion of Norway, he's at his best in the long hard classics and a powerful hitter with a chance to pull off a win on any given day. Licence to seek out stage wins without any specific assisting role but will be expected to provide pace and effort to aid the team effort when required.

103: Mark Cavendish. The fastest man in the world. The World Champion. The quickest sprinter in this, or any race, and the most prolific stage winner riding. Still only 27 and already the winner of twenty stages. Here to add to those, but unsure of how much support he can rely on from a team committed to winning the overall prize.

104: Bernie Eisel. Cav's right-hand man. Mark Cavendish brought his trusty lieutenant with him to Team Sky from the engine room of their HTC squad after plundering Tour wins together for years. The motor-mouthed Austrian is a massively popular member of the team and expected to single-handedly do the job a whole team did last year and lead Cav out.

105: Chris Froome. The secret weapon. The African-bred Brit climbed to a completely unpredicted second place in last year's Vuelta a España, as good as any result by a British cyclist in a grand tour in the history of cycling. Here, his job is to accompany Wiggins every step of the way in the mountains, and provide a Plan B if the sideburned Plan A doesn't pan out.

106: Christian Knees. The horse. Sean Yates would never want to take an army into battle without at least one man to do his old job. Get on the front. Raise the tempo. Close things down. Put some hurt on. With a man like Knees on the front, the others can take a break, knowing the lanky German will do the work of ten men if necessary.

107: Richie Porte. The class act. The young Australian has carried out his apprenticeship alongside Alberto Contador at Saxo Bank and is ready to become the hitter he has always promised to be. Strong in the time trial and when things curve uphill, he has all the attributes to be a leader of a grand tour team himself. This year, he is one of those whom Wiggins will look to lean on in the Alps and Pyrenees, and a possible Plan C.

108: Mick Rogers. The captain. Three times the World Time Trial Champion, the 32-year-old from New South Wales has always been known for his wise head. Briefly a contender himself when leading the T-Mobile and HTC squads, his role as decision-maker on the road for Wiggins and the rest sits comfortably on his experienced shoulders. Will be expected to be one of the pace-setters on the lower slopes of the big climbs.

109: Kanstantsin Siutsou. The pro. The Belarusian has been on the scene since becoming World Under-23 Champion in 2004, picking up stage wins and overall places in the grand tours ever since. Impressed Team Sky while at HTC last year when his prodigious climbing dragged Wiggins back up to

Evans and Vinokourov in the Dauphiné Libéré when the Brit was in danger of losing the lead. Will form part of a powerful climbing phalanx with Froome, Porte and Rogers to fight for Wiggins in the mountains.

★

The route from Visé to Tournai is a flat rush over 200-odd kilometres of bleak Flanders lowland. The day will be characterised by the non-sprinters trying to escape the bunch and the sprinters' teams trying to pull them back and set up a sprint. Therefore, there are two guarantees about today's racing: it will be really fast, and it will be dangerous.

Team Sky will want to win today. Mark Cavendish will really want to win. This is the sort of day that will probably be known by future generations as a Cav Day, a day where it feels that whatever anyone does, there is only going to be one winner. Flat sprint stages often have this feel of inevitability after they've finished, but in the heat of battle it's clear that, in truth, anything can and probably will happen.

The teams that have come to this race with hopes of a sprint victory are:

Orica-GreenEDGE. The newly formed Australian team is built on the Team Sky blueprint, using a well-established national track programme as a springboard for road success. For now, though, they lack a leader to challenge for the overall prize. They are here to look for opportunistic stage wins through the likes of adventurers like Simon Gerrans, old stager Stuart O'Grady, and their most successful rider of the spring, Michael Albasini. But they also have a tasty fast man: Matt Goss. No, not that guy out of Bros, the one who has been leading out Cav at HTC for a couple of years.

Lotto Belisol. The Belgian-based classics team have Mark Cavendish's greatest rival in their sprint plans, the speedy German André Greipel. No love is lost between these two, with Greipel having to play second fiddle to Cavendish at various team incarnations for much of his early career. The German believes that he can beat Cavendish, that he can beat the World Champion in a straight *mano-a-mano* battle and, sometimes, he can. But not often.

Liquigas-Cannondale. The Italians have discovered a rare talent in yesterday's stage winner and early wearer of the green jersey for most consistent finisher, Peter Sagan. Though Cavendish has greater pure speed than the Slovakian *arriviste*, Sagan's ability to score on all sorts of terrain makes him a formidable obstacle if the green jersey is to go back to the Isle of Man like last year.

Lampre-ISD. Alessandro Petacchi used to be really fast, one of the few men to give Mario Cipollini a regular hiding when the Lion King was at his peak. The key phrase here is 'used to be'. One wonders why they bother with all the chasing and the leading out when Petacchi is clearly devoid of the oomph he once displayed on a daily basis.

Garmin-Sharp. Despite contesting Tour de France sprint finishes for many years, Tyler Farrar boasts a grand total of one stage win versus his contemporary Cavendish's twenty. Still, Garmin–Sharp gamely do their bit and lead him out every time, surely more in hope than expectation.

These are the main players in the last 20km of a flat stage, as they fight to keep the race together and position their designated strikers for the final dash to the line.

Today, everybody from Team Sky remains upright, the best feeling of all for Dave Brailsford, who knows that for all his talk of attention to detail and marginal gains, no amount of preparation can fix a problem like last year's withdrawal of their leader after kissing the tarmac at high speed.

Into the last 20km and Edvald Boasson Hagen and Mark Cavendish are in the mix for Team Sky, but there is no sign of a long train of teammates leading out the Manx Missile as would have been expected if this were 2011 and he was wearing the white jersey of HTC. Instead, the two Team Sky riders wearing white jerseys – Cav's with the rainbow bands of

World Champion and Boasson Hagen's with the Norwegian flag as national title-holder – are fighting for themselves to hold their places near the front of the breathtakingly fast peloton as it snakes towards Tournai across the battlefields of the Great War. Team Sky have revived a long-forgotten Tour tradition denoting the leading team on overall classification by donning yellow headwear. Evoking memories of Anquetil or Merckx and their teammates in yellow cotton caps, the Team Sky riders are wearing helmets in the same colour as Cancellara's leader's jersey. It is an unfamiliar look, but it makes it easier to pick out Boasson Hagen and Cav as they jockey in the speeding pack.

Lotto Belisol are dominant, a full train of riders pumping their legs in harmony like the Mallard hauling an express train at record speed. Greipel is in pole position as they head under the red kite that signifies the last kilometre. Sagan is crouching his big frame to stay on the German's wheel, hoping to be able to blast away from him like Chris Hoy on the track when they approach the line. Cav is further back, without conspicuous teammates, but following the experienced Óscar Freire. 'I knew that there was some headwind and it was clear to me that I could also have a chance if I started from a bit further back,' explained Cavendish regarding his positioning. 'I knew Freire always goes up in the last kilometre so I stayed with him.'

Greipel explodes off his teammate Greg Henderson's wheel with 200m remaining and Sagan has no reply to the acceleration. However, there's somebody else bearing down on the German – his nemesis, the World Champion. Greipel has his wish, a head-to-head battle to prove who is the fastest man in this race, a chance for one or other to prove his credentials as cycling's Usain Bolt.

Only the first part of Greipel's dream comes true. Cavendish's front wheel breaks the finish line a fraction of a second before his, and sprinting is not a game for celebrating second place.

Bradley Wiggins, Fabian Cancellara and all the main rivals are home safely, so Brad still sits quietly in second place, seven seconds separating him from the Swiss leader. All is going to plan.

Mark Cavendish has won 21 stages of the greatest race on Earth, and win number 21 came without the assistance of his team. Does this prove that there is harmony within the Team Sky household as they try to win on two fronts? We probably won't know the answer to that until one of their twin objectives becomes thwarted. What if there is a sprint stage and Cavendish gets beaten? What if Wiggins gets caught out because his teammates are concentrating on earning Cavendish a stage win? At present, the latter scenario looks highly unlikely, as the overall objective remains crystal clear. What is more probable is that there will be a chance to see if the Manx rider can keep his famously fiery disposition in check if things don't go his way.

★

Wiggins and Cavendish go back – a long way back. They have roomed together for years on national duty at Olympics and World Championships, and nearly ended up as professional teammates at T-Mobile back when the latter was first scaring the established order of sprinters and the former was being groomed as a *rouleur* to add horsepower on the flat and lead out the fast men. It is perhaps surprising then, that it wasn't until Brad was in his thirties that they actually joined each other on a professional team, and by then one of them was champion of the world and the other one was a genuine Tour de France contender. Their separate goals don't seem to have separated them. Based on huge mutual appreciation for their differing strengths, their comradeship is natural and without hierarchy. Wiggins famously does impressions of his brasher teammate to entertain the others, while Cavendish pretends to ridicule Wiggins's guitar skills. The trick for the Team Sky backroom is to ensure that this goodwill continues. The management would surely be the first department to feel any anger from either party if things don't work out: they like each other too much to blame each other for a falling out.

⊙

THE BARCELONA OLYMPICS UNDERSTANDABLY didn't grip the country in quite the same way that London 2012 held our attention, but they were a major occasion nonetheless. For the best part of a week, we gasped at the opulence of the opening ceremony, sighed at the dramatic backdrop of the beautiful city behind the high dive board and listened to Freddie Mercury and Dame Montserrat Caballé blasting out the theme tune.

But we craved a gold medal.

The athletics hadn't started yet, so we were still waiting for Linford Christie and Sally Gunnell to take the stage. The so-called 'minor sports' had held sway for the opening few days and the country developed a passionate interest in sailing, archery and rowing. It was very exciting, but what we needed was a hero. We found him in an unlikely shape.

Chris Boardman was known as The Professor. The studious approach he had developed alongside his coach and mentor, Peter Keen, became synonymous with his name throughout his cycling career, but the first time he entered the general public consciousness was here in Barcelona. Their Teutonic application to the 4,000 metre individual pursuit had left no stone unturned in the hunt for perfection and victory, least of all the bike he would ride.

A slightly more British character was Mike Burrows, the archetypal mad inventor. Despite looking more like a member of Pink Floyd than Dr Snuggles, Burrows had turned his formidable mind to making the world's most effective racing bike. Lotus had then built it out of carbon fibre for Boardman, and as a result the country found itself cooing over a bicycle that, to them, looked more at home on board the USS *Enterprise* than underneath a district nurse.

On a hot August evening in Catalonia, Chris Boardman saddled up against the reigning World Champion Jens Lehmann of Germany. He may have shared a name with his countryman and latterly madcap Arsenal goalkeeper, but there was nothing inconsistent about this German: he was the real deal. Could the boy from Hoylake on the Wirral overthrow him at this, the pinnacle of sporting goals, the Olympics?

Nobody was watching more intently than a fascinated twelve-year-old boy in Paddington. Glued to the telly with his mum, Bradley Wiggins couldn't believe his eyes. The skinsuit, the aero helmet, but most of all, that amazing bike. He wanted one. He wanted to be that man in that helmet on that bike.

Brad sat rapt as the commentator explained the intricacies of the pursuit. The two men would start on opposite sides of the track then head off, each on their own 4km time trial. At the line, the faster man would be the gold medallist, except in the unlikely event that one rider caught the other, then the race would be over. Nobody ever caught each other at this sort of level though; they were all simply too good for that.

Boardman caught Lehmann. It was extraordinary. A country rejoiced, a nation had its gold medal, and one tall skinny twelve-year-old in West London had a dream – to be an Olympic gold medal-winning cyclist.

Sally Gunnell, Linford Christie, Steve Redgrave and Matthew Pinsent all paraded across the same television screen in the coming days. By the time the closing ceremony lit up the Catalonian sky, Bradley was mesmerised. Hooked for good. Dreams of playing in goal for Arsenal disappeared into the ether due, ironically, to the defeat of Jens Lehmann in Barcelona.

To this day, Brad is unsure whether Linda simply supported her boy's new-found enthusiasm for the sport, or whether she cunningly led him down the path before he'd even known he was walking upon it. She'd called him in to watch that broadcast of Boardman from his kickabout downstairs. She organised a trip out to the Hayes Bypass, a curious bit of new road that was being extended into Middlesex where, until it was completed, local cyclists would charge up and down in organised races. On his old Halfords bike and a ridiculously old-fashioned helmet of his dad's discovered in granddad's shed, the eager teen rode his first event. In the second one he came third.

Linda ran into a familiar face one week: Stuart Benstead, the local man who had introduced Garry to the London bike scene when he had arrived from Australia. Now Brad had somebody who could help him make sense of the arcane mysteries of bike racing, and Stuart had a prodigious young talent to nurture. It was a good match for both of them. Brad joined the local club, the Archer Road Club, and began to ride on the old track at Herne Hill.

His first proper racing bike, a Ribble from Lancashire, was purchased but only with the compensation money that came about after his first proper accident. Brad was expecting a strong lesson from Linda, but his mum instead turned her wrath upon the woman who had carelessly knocked him off on the way to club night.

Bike events were a strange world in those days, full of dispassionate men who were passionate about bike racing. There were more bobbly old tracksuit tops and clipboards than you could shake a pump at. Brad worked his way steadily up through the ranks of the various events and age groups, trying most track disciplines and getting some good road rides in, heading out of the city with the club to the leafy lanes of Buckinghamshire and Berkshire. He went to his first National Championships in Manchester aged fifteen and came home as National Schoolboy Points Champion, an event he hadn't regarded as his forte. By then he was convinced that his future lay in professional cycling, and that's what he was going to do. He loved riding his bike, but he wanted to make money out of it, too, not play at it. He saw it as his best chance of making a good life for himself. He got himself on to the national junior squad with another good run of performances at the following year's championships and was now on track to be a cyclist.

Which was lucky, because he'd completely lost interest in education. School had fizzled out and a lacklustre enrolment on a business studies course ended prematurely after racing got in the way of lectures.

It looked like Bradley Wiggins had no choice. He would have to be a bike racer.

Orchies–Boulogne-sur-Mer, 197km
Tuesday, 3 July 2012

Second place in the prologue and second place overall for Bradley Wiggins mean Team Sky have had a relatively relaxed first couple of days on the Tour de France. It has fallen upon the leader Fabian Cancellara's RadioShack-Nissan team to do all the hard yards at the front of the race to ensure their man stays in yellow for as long as possible. As they are well aware that Cancellara's leadership of the race is certain to end in the mountains, it's the perfect arrangement as far as Team Sky are concerned. What's more, their prolific stage winner, Mark Cavendish, has already given them a victory, and they didn't even have to do anything to help him. It all adds up to a dream start.

Today will be a wake-up call.

Kanstantsin Siutsou is not one of the most prominent members of this squad. If people were likely to say 'Who?' about anybody when the team revealed their nine men for the Tour de France, it would have been about the Belarusian. For heaven's sake, we weren't even sure how to write his name: he was often Constantine Sivtsov in race results and remained Kanstantsin Sivtsov at his previous team, HTC.

When the Team Sky hierarchy sat down to figure out the final line-up for Liège, most of the names picked themselves. They weren't going to go without Wiggins, Froome, Porte or Rogers; they were the men who would form the mountain commando unit charged with bringing home yellow. They would surely take Edvald Boasson Hagen. The Norwegian's all-round power would be enough to make him leader of many rival teams. They hadn't spent that money on Mark Cavendish to leave the rainbow jersey hanging in a cupboard in Douglas. The seventh spot would go to Cavendish's lieutenant, Bernie Eisel, brought from HTC with his boss for this exact purpose. There would have to be a *rouleur* that could be relied upon to do the donkey work, day in day out, especially if everything went to plan and the team found themselves defending the yellow jersey for many days. The team was spoilt for choice in this department, with Ian Stannard and Matt Hayman fancied by many outside the team, but the metronomic Christian Knees got the nod from those in the know. Who would be the last member? Geraint Thomas had been a revelation in last year's race, taking the fight to the opposition after Wiggins had been dumped out of the contest. He had also been indefatigable in the classics, where his efforts in the jersey of GB Champion were appreciated by Boasson Hagen and Juan Antonio Flecha. Rigoberto Urán Urán was surely worth a spot for his glorious name alone, never mind his sterling efforts for the team in just about every performance he had made over the last two years. In the end, the Olympic team pursuit squad would be Thomas's goal, and Urán Urán would ride both the Giro and the Vuelta so a third grand tour was out of the question for the young Colombian.

To see why Siutsou got the call, we need to go back to the Critérium du Dauphiné of 2011. An important goal in itself, June's Dauphiné has long been the destination of Tour de France hopefuls fine-tuning their form. Previously known as the Dauphiné Libéré, it was here in the south of France and the Alps that Miguel Indurain used to test himself against his rivals a month before the battle proper. Bradley Wiggins won the prestigious event in 2011, beating eventual Tour winner Cadel Evans in the process. Not without a scare, however.

Stage 11 of this Tour de France will not be the first time Brad has battled the Alpine giant of La Toussuire. While wearing the leader's jersey on these slopes in the 2011 Dauphiné, Brad was subjected to a brutal attack by Joaquin Rodriguez and

Cadel Evans that put his lead at severe risk. Wiggins, like Evans, prefers to use his remarkable engine to control his speed on the slopes of big climbs; neither of them enjoys the jerkier stop-start attacks of pure climbers like Rodriguez, known as Il Puro for his cigar-like shape. Brad prefers to let moves go and grind out the yards separating him from his tormentor until he drags himself back into contention. This attack, however, was the real deal. A real gap had opened up and the jersey was sliding off his shoulders. Ever calm, he set about the task of nullifying the move, but he needed some help.

It came in the unlikely shape of Kanstantsin Siutsou. The HTC man had first hit the headlines in 2004 when he delighted all of Belarus by taking the World Under-23 Road Championship. Since then, he had carved out a decent, if unspectacular career for himself, winning his national jersey and stages in races like the Giro d'Italia. Looking back, though, it was his strong showing in the overall classification of big races that really demonstrated the sort of rider he had become: winning the Tour de Georgia and cementing top twenty finishes at both the Tour de France and the Giro. He was a *rouleur* with a big engine who could lay it down in the mountains, and that's what he did right there and then on Toussuire.

There were rumours that an on-the-spot offer was made of a contract with Team Sky if he pulled it out for Wiggins that day, but stories like that abound in cycling. What is more certain is that when La Toussuire appeared in the roadbook of the 2012 Tour de France, everyone at Team Sky would have remembered how the experienced Belarusian had ridden there a year before. He rode alongside Wiggins for the 2012 Dauphiné where the Brit retained his title, and also during his successful assault on Switzerland's Tour de Romandie. Siutsou was well worth his place in the nine. Which is why it was so disappointing that he became the first rider to abandon the 2012 Tour de France.

We've heard a lot about crashes in the first week of the Tour, but this wasn't really what we had in mind. This was not some crazy snarl-up in the last few kilometres as everybody rides flat out to hold their place or move up the line, or a death-defying descent in torrential rain. With 50km to go in a fairly typical northern stage, there was a touch of wheels and Siutsou hit the deck hard enough to break his tibia. It happens. But that doesn't make it easier to bear for you or your team when you are the victim.

After that, the crashes come thick and fast. The roads of this stage are narrower than the first two, as the organisers attempt to take the race up some smaller local climbs, and the attendant nervousness spreads. Team Sky group around Wiggins, and Yates and Rogers are adamant that they need to ride at the front, the safest place in the bunch.

However, as Chris Froome would later ruefully point out, 'You can't have 200 riders on the front though.' With the finish atop a sharp little rise similar to the springboard Peter Sagan had used for victory on Stage 1, everybody was desperate to be at the head of things. Into the frantic final kilometre, and Wiggins and his entourage are within touching distance of the front when the experienced Katusha sprinter Óscar Freire is squeezed into the barriers directly in front of them, bringing everybody on the left-hand side of the road to a standstill. Brad was able to clip out of his pedals and stop, but Froome found himself straddling the barriers in an effort to avoid hitting the deck.

Panic quickly subsided when it was clear that nobody else had been injured, and the riders, shaken by Siutsou's exit, calmly proceeded to the line. Bradley's second spot was protected by the Tour rule that dictates all riders delayed by a crash in the final kilometre shall be given the same time as the bunch they were in when it happened. Phew.

In front of them, Sylvain Chavanel was trying to ride roughshod over that, anyway. The Frenchman, level on time with Wiggins, launched a ferocious attack to try and win on the slopes into Boulogne. If he could finish one second clear of the bunch, second place overall would be his. If it could be eight seconds, then the *maillot jaune* itself would be his. He hadn't reckoned on the awesome power of the 21-year-old Liquigas-Cannondale Slovak though, and Peter Sagan soared clear with immense power to take his second great stage and solidify his grasp on the green jersey. Behind him, our hero Edvald smashed his way to the finish line to take second place, with the yellow jersey of Switzerland's own tough guy, Fabian Cancellara, just behind him.

Team Sky retreat to the Big Black Bus to consider the day, lick their wounds, consider their losses and count their blessings. They're a man down, but the hitters survived some scares. They could have lost a serious chunk of time if the big pile-up had happened a couple of minutes earlier. Breathe steadily. Move on.

Sean Yates speaks to *Sky Sports* about Kanstantsin Siutsou. 'He is a big loss. We have to deal with it. It will just impact on the workload of the other seven members of the team.'

Non-cycling followers watching Sky Sports News furrow their brows. 'I thought he just said they were down to eight riders? Now he's talking about seven?' Of course, for Yates, it's obvious that there is one rider who won't lift a finger unless he has to: Bradley Wiggins. He is here to win and must be protected and assisted at every turn.

And then there were eight. As Yates says: 'One minute all is calm, the next minute all hell is let loose. It's a little bit nerve-racking.'

REALLY, THERE USED TO be only one way to be a full-time cyclist. You had to join a team and be a professional road rider. There were the odd few who would go to Europe and live off scraps at sponsored amateurs and hope that their results would bring them that pro contract, or an even more select band that Bradley Wiggins's father, Garry, had tried to break into who could make a living out of the European winter indoor track circuit, but even they would usually supplement their income by riding on a pro team in the summer.

In the 1970s and 1980s there was quite a tidy home-based professional scene. Based largely upon criteriums, town centre racing that would take place on evenings throughout the summer months, and the round-Britain Milk Race, there was a fair amount of cash to be had. Riders like Keith 'Leggo' Lambert and Sid Barras grafted hard for their wins and led powerful teams of tough pros. They were professional sportsmen and, if not salaried like today's sports stars, they could earn a good living and be counted alongside the footballers, cricketers and rugby league stars of their day. Rugby league is actually a good comparison, as, like rugby, cycling had a seismic split down the middle. Professionals and amateurs. Never the twain shall meet. The amateurs had their racing scene, with the peak being the amateur National and World Championships and the Olympic and Commonwealth Games, while the professionals had an entirely different calendar.

Great British riders of the era like Chris Walker, Malcolm Elliott or Sean Yates were unable to illuminate the Olympics at their peak, because they were pros. A serial UK winner like Chris Lillywhite, now working alongside his old teammate Shane Sutton as part of the GB set-up, turned professional at seventeen and never got a sniff of the Olympic rings. The great Sean Kelly had been pre-selected for Ireland to go to the Montreal Olympics but was caught racing in apartheid South Africa under an assumed name for money and turfed out, causing him to turn professional earlier than intended.

Two things changed to unite the sport during the 1990s. Firstly, the Olympics became 'open'. Anybody could enter regardless of their professional status. The traditionalists argued that the amateur ethos of sport for its own sake was irreparably damaged, while the reformers retorted that as a celebration of the best in sport, the Olympics should feature the best sportsmen and women. Whatever the rights and wrongs, the deed was done, and people like Miguel Indurain, Tim Henman and Ryan Giggs became, largely to their own surprise and delight, Olympic athletes. It meant that the Olympics were no longer a sideshow in cycling, they were part of the main event, and professional careers could be tilted towards the medal podium.

The other big change was the introduction of National Lottery funding. Amateur sports that had always been the backbone of the Olympic programme like athletics, swimming and cycling had always relied on dedicated individuals prepared to go to breaking point in their home and family lives, foregoing work or relaxation in return for squeezing training in somewhere and somehow. This had ultimately resulted in Great Britain's worst return at a modern Olympics in 1996, when Steve Redgrave and Matthew Pinsent's brilliant victory represented the country's only gold medal of the Games. UK Sport was established the year after the Atlanta Games, with the responsibility of distributing money raised via the National Lottery to fund sport.

As well as promoting grass roots schemes and growing public participation in sport and exercise, the stated aims in UK Sport were to increase the number of medals at Olympics and World Championships. This was revolutionary for cycling, as Chris Boardman's coach Peter Keen and his successor Dave Brailsford were able to establish the phenomenally successful track cycling programme that won so many medals at Athens, Beijing and London, and turn Great Britain into the world's most successful track cycling nation.

One of the ways they did this was to pay a stipend to athletes likely to make the grade to enable them to train and prepare properly without going to work. In other words, a cyclist could now make a living without having to choose between turning professional or going to the Olympics.

The seventeen-year-old Bradley Wiggins had been dreaming of the Olympics for five years after seeing Chris Boardman make them his own in 1992. He went to the National Junior

Track Championships and won the 3,000m pursuit, the scratch race, the points race and the 1km time trial. He was also making waves in the Pete Buckley Trophy, a national series of road races for juniors. It gained him selection for the World Junior Championships in Cape Town, a high honour for a rider's first year in the juniors, and a berth that had often been left empty in previous years as the expense of sending a team was weighed against the likelihood of success. Brad finished sixteenth in the individual pursuit and then a wonderful fourth in the points race behind the man who would one day be his road captain at Team Sky, Mick Rogers.

Coaching, training and diet became Brad's new life. He had had a taste of how things could be in South Africa and he wasn't about to let that life slip through his fingers for want of application. He ate, drank and breathed cycling, and by his own admission must have been a very boring teenager. A year after Cape Town, he was on a plane for Havana for his second Junior Worlds, a year older, a year stronger, a year wiser. With that in mind, another fourth spot in the points race was a huge disappointment, and the eighteen-year-old was crushed by what he perceived as his failure. The team management persuaded him to have a crack at the pursuit, which he saw as his weaker event. Amazingly relaxed and pressure-free after the expectation of the points race, Bradley sailed through the rounds and 'before I knew it I had won the bloody title' as he later described in *In Pursuit of Glory*.

And before he knew it, the Junior World Champion was in Kuala Lumpur with the senior England squad for the Commonwealth Games and was winning a silver medal as part of a hastily rejigged team pursuit squad. The five-man squad from which the quartet of riders were chosen was comprised of Bradley Wiggins, Matt Illingworth, Colin Sturgess, Jonny Clay and Rob Hayles. They represented the best of Great Britain as well as England, and Bradley knew only too well what that meant: a place at the Olympics was in his grasp. With only two years until Sydney, he was part of the best team pursuit squad this country had ever produced, running the all-conquering Australians close in Malaysia, with the best yet to come.

That wasn't even the sum of 1998's good news. UK Cycling took their new Lottery money from UK Sport and gave £20,000 of it to Brad to allow him to train properly and prepare to win medals for his country.

There was a new star in the firmament.

Abbeville–Rouen, 214.5km
Wednesday, 4 July 2012

The road to Rouen is paved with uncertainty. Crashes, crashes, crashes: the story of the first week in the Tour de France for many years. Is it getting worse? Or is it the fact that we have a man in this race with the hopes and dreams of a nation riding on his shoulders? Is that why we watch with white knuckles gripping the armchair? We're dreading '*Chute dans le peloton!*' to be swiftly followed by '101, Wiggins.'

It doesn't help that we've been here before. It is a fact of cycling that people who crash tend to crash again. They don't necessarily cause crashes – though some do – but they don't have the supernatural awareness some have which helps them avoid the accidents when they happen. As somebody who has crashed out of this event once already, concerns run high for Bradley Wiggins.

Mark Cavendish is no stranger to ripped shorts either. He has been accused of being reckless by his sprinting opponents, and, when he was younger perhaps, they may have had a point. These days, his problems in the sprint tend to stem from fearlessness rather than recklessness, as he continues to put his nose in where it hurts and take the risks needed to win races. Being the most marked man in the sport brings its own dangers, too, as rivals fight to get on the wheel of the fastest finisher. In a sprint stage, if you finish in front of Cav, you probably win the race. More insidiously, there are those who will actively try to baulk him, as the Italian sprinter Roberto Ferrari did in May's Giro d'Italia. Ferrari callously flicked off his line when he sensed Cavendish beginning to overtake him in the classic 'switch' – the most underhand and despised of all sprinting misdemeanours. At an estimated 75kph, with no protective clothing other than a skid lid, the World Champion was lucky to get up from that crash and continue in the race.

It wasn't his only crash in the Giro, either. One problem riders don't have to contend with on the Tour as much as its Italian counterpart is corners. The Giro organisers love a 90-degree bend 200m from the line. At least the Tour bosses realise that this is probably a bad idea if you want to keep your competitors alive, even if a smattering of road furniture and roundabouts in the final run-in are often unavoidable. The beauty of road cycling as a sport is that it takes place on public roads that we can all use. The downfall of road cycling as a sport is that it takes place on public roads that we all know have bends, potholes, bumps and narrow bits.

You can guess where this is leading to . . .

Brad avoided today's big smash, but Cav didn't, and neither did his constant companion Bernie Eisel, who was naturally alongside him at the time. With numerous abrasions and a damaged hand, the World Champion rolled over the line a few minutes after the stage winner, but within that small vignette was contained his most painful injury: André Greipel had won the stage. The German was definitely the fastest in this sprint in the absence of his more garlanded former teammate and took the prize accordingly. This made Cavendish as livid as the rips in his jersey and shorts, and the blood dripping down his battered body. The fact that Alessandro Petacchi had finished second just showed him that, in his mind, taking his 22nd Tour stage would have been like removing sweets from the proverbial toddler.

'We see this kind of thing time and time again,' Sean Yates wearily told the Sky News reporters at the finish. 'Nobody wants to see crashes for anybody and we were among the victims again today.'

Somebody else who, perhaps surprisingly, decided to have a public opinion on the accident was Mark Cavendish's girlfriend. Peta Todd took to Twitter to declare imperiously, 'This is people's lives. If you haven't got the intention of making sure you have the team to look after the World Champ don't just wing it. He is just a man.'

The Team Sky hierarchy's reaction to being lectured on tactics by a Page 3 glamour model sadly went unrecorded. Questioned about Todd's comments, Dave Brailsford shrugged and said, 'Sprinters crash, that's just part and parcel of the job.' He could have swapped 'Cavendish crashes' for 'Sprinters crash', but we knew what he meant.

It is interesting to reflect on what Team Sky could have done differently to keep Cavendish out of such a crash when he was fighting for position in the run-in to a finish that he fancied. Or perhaps Todd blames all his teams for all her boyfriend's crashes over the years? What seemed more likely is that this was an opportunity to let off some steam about the more general issue: that, for once, Mark Cavendish was not the star of the show. Team Sky were here to make Bradley Wiggins the first British winner of the Tour de France, not retain Mark Cavendish's green jersey of best sprinter. Surely Cavendish, and by extension his partner, must have known that when he signed for Team Sky?

To follow the logic of Todd's rather rambling tweet, Team Sky should either build their team around Cavendish or not include him in their nine selected riders. We can only imagine what her reaction would have been if they had left him out of their Tour de France team. And Team Sky's stated mission was to win the Tour de France with a British rider. Seriously, what did the Cavendish camp think? And what did Cavendish think when he heard about the row? Did he close his eyes and inwardly groan? Did he feel a warm glow of pride at hearing his partner support him so staunchly? Did he even discuss it with her beforehand, perhaps a subtle way of letting the world know how he felt without upsetting Team Sky's precariously balanced apple cart?

Those of us with an interest in modern sport know how Twitter can bring comradeship, enlightenment and understanding to its participants, or instant opprobrium crashing down on the heads of those who use it unwisely. Goodness knows how many times Kevin Pietersen's friends, family and teammates must have wanted to wrench his iPhone out of his hands and smash it into a million pieces before he bashed out another self-destructive 140 characters.

Several of Team Sky's riders' partners are regular tweeters. It would seem likely that many of their followers do so because of the identity of their husbands and boyfriends rather than any personal prowess, though Todd's modelling career has of course brought her plenty of fans of her own. This race still has more than two weeks to go, and the action hasn't even started in earnest yet.

THE EIGHTEEN-YEAR-OLD BRADLEY WIGGINS sat down at Christmas 1998 and thought about his future. He didn't need any motivation to achieve his immediate goal: to go to the Sydney Olympics in 2000. He'd been dreaming about it since his first laps round his flats in 1992 as a twelve-year-old Boardman fan. He knew that to make this happen, he would have to be motivated enough to make 1999 a very hard year indeed. He would need the results to keep him in the frame for selection for Sydney and grow from being one of the world's best juniors into a man.

After Sydney, he would choose from one of the teams that had begun to follow his progress and turn professional, leave the track for the road and become a Tour de France rider. Those had been his twin ambitions ever since he'd begun racing in earnest at Herne Hill and on the Hayes Bypass: the Olympics and the Tour.

He settled in well with the Great Britain track squad after his baptism with the big boys in Kuala Lumpur. The professionalism of the track squad was growing year on year and the new line-up for the 1999 World Championships in Berlin reflected that. Brad, Paul Manning, Bryan Steele, Matt Illingworth and Rob Hayles largely represented the new breed of Lottery-funded full-time athletes whose goal was medals at the World Championships and the Olympics. They would tackle the team pursuit in a better-prepared state than any team before them.

They were fifth in Berlin, a good result reflecting an upward curve in performance from previous World Championships, and the team and management firmly believed in their medal chances at the Games in a year's time. Rob Hayles and Brad also rode the madison in Berlin where they did well enough to suggest they could take the partnership to Sydney. They would need to keep at it and avoid injury, but it looked like Brad was now a shoo-in for Olympic selection.

The winter of 1999 was a strange and exciting time for Bradley Wiggins. In their quest to ride well in the Olympic madison, he and Rob Hayles decided to have a crack at the six-day circuit. Here, there were many echoes of his absent father, and he met many people who remembered his dad, with reactions ranging through horror via fright all the way to affection.

The Olympic squad formed in earnest in January 2000. Matt Illingworth had clashed with the coach Simon Jones over the team's preparation and training methods, and as the most senior member of the squad felt as though he should have some sway. Jones was keen to be seen as his own man and there was only going to be one winner, especially as Illingworth's replacement turned out to be the star of the domestic road scene, Chris Newton.

By the time they got to Sydney seven months later, the newly GB-suited squad had been through a punishing year during which they had been drilled to within an inch of their lives. The enormity of the Games was hard to take in for Bradley and he was relieved that the team opted out of the opening ceremony as the team pursuit was to take place at the beginning of the Games programme. He was in danger of becoming terminally star-struck and needed to focus.

Atlanta was put to bed on the very first night, when Jason Queally muscled his way to an amazing gold medal in the very first event, the 1km time trial. The whole track squad went berserk – they knew their confidence was not misplaced and they could take on the world.

The team pursuit squad went through their solid preparation routine and minutely planned changeovers and speed control in their first round. Jones's coaching was justified by the setting of a new Olympic record. The excited team took a breather before their quarter-final later that same night. They cruised past the Netherlands into the semi-finals. A medal, so far out of reach in this event for so many years, was within touching distance.

It wasn't going to be gold, though. The Ukrainians, favourites for this event after their World Championship showings over recent seasons, took a whole two seconds out of the GB quartet, who were still able to beat the British record in that same ride. Unbowed by losing to a better team, they went back out and beat the British record again in defeating France for the bronze. Bradley Wiggins was an Olympic medallist.

Rob Hayles's crash in the madison a few days later, to whom no blame could be attached after other riders ricocheted into him, robbed the pair of another medal. Brad hung in without his partner for the final laps to ensure they got fourth, but it was a disappointment. Not one large enough to dampen the joy that bronze had brought, though. The Olympic medal Brad had dreamed of since he was a boy was his and he could now turn professional and say goodbye to the track career that had served him so well.

Or would he? Sydney had left such an impression on Bradley Wiggins that the image of that Olympic flame remained burned on to his retinas. How could he turn his back on that? He realised that at twenty years old, he could conceivably see competition at another three or even four Olympics if he was able to maintain or improve on the level he'd reached. He immediately began wondering about the possibilities of Athens 2004 and whether he could combine those goals with a successful career on the roads of Europe.

There was an ideal step waiting for the returning Olympian. In tandem with Great Britain's progress on the track, there was now a British professional team racing on the continent. The 1990s had been a dark time for British cycling. The demise of the last team to take on the Europeans at their own game, ANC-Halfords in 1987 in a scandalous mess, had hit the scene hard, and only isolated rides by the likes of Sean Yates and Malcolm Elliott shone. Compared to the 1980s when Robert Millar had ridden to the King of the Mountains jersey and fourth place in the Tour de France, the Kellogg's Tour of Britain had attracted millions to the roadside and the Irish neighbours Sean Kelly and Stephen Roche were dominating world cycling, it was slim pickings.

But an unusual thing had happened. An ideas man from Kent by the name of Julian Clark had persuaded the McCartney family that a vegetarian British cycling team would be the ideal promotional vehicle for Linda McCartney Foods, the vegetarian ready meals business run by the ex-Beatle's charismatic wife. In their second year, 1999, Clark had managed to persuade British number one Max Sciandri and Swiss legend Pascal Richard to front his burgeoning team. The pair had taken bronze and gold medals respectively in that first open Olympic road race in Atlanta. With the Olympic Champion on board and a host of eager fresh faces, Linda McCartney even managed to get an invite to the 2000 Giro d'Italia. It got even better for the exciting popular newcomers when the flinty Australian David McKenzie won the stage from Vasto to Teramo with a scarcely believable 164km lone break that had won the hearts of the Italian public. And it was all pulled off under the tutelage of a man in his first year of cycling management. After landing something of a coup in persuading Sean Yates out of retirement to ride the 1998 Tour of Britain as a guest Linda McCartney rider, Julian Clark had made the legendary Brit sporting director of the team.

Things could only get better for the Linda McCartney team. They brought in Jacob's Creek and Jaguar as co-sponsors for 2001 and set upon an ambitious expansion plan, bringing in Spanish hitters like Juan Carlos Domínguez and Íñigo Cuesta, and exciting young signings such as the former World Junior Road Champion, Mark Scanlon from Ireland. They also brought in a co-director to accompany Yates in the form of Neil Stephens, the popular recently retired Australian.

There was one signing that made more headlines than any others, though. The new star of British cycling, the twenty-year-old Sydney bronze medallist Bradley Wiggins, was joining.

It seemed like the ideal move for Wiggins. An English-speaking team would integrate him into European cycling more gently than the established Euro powerhouses. This was an exciting new squad who were sweeping away preconceptions about 'old school' cycling and made a big deal about being clean and drug free, one where friendly faces like Matt Stephens and Russell Downing would be. The Tour de France was just a few more eye-catching rides away for the new squad, perhaps even in 2001.

The money was right, and Bradley was assisted by his old friend and sometime manager Richard Allchin in settling the deal. Hands were shaken. Cars were loaded. Brad drove himself down to the team's new base in Toulouse and began to pin up posters of *The Italian Job*, The Who and Muhammad Ali around his rather pokey little billet in Colomiers. However, it proved to be a miserable month. The bulk of the team were in Australia riding the team's first race of the year, the Tour Down Under, and there was nothing much for the twenty-year-old to do other than ride his bike. Christmas Day 2000 in Haute-Garonne was warm and sunny with the peaks of the distant Pyrenees pricking the blue horizon. But by mid-January, a familiar soggy fog had settled over the sweetcorn fields that took the more enthusiastic rider out beyond the Forêt de Bouconne and the sleepy villages of Gers. It was a bedraggled and solitary Wiggins who arrived in Bagshot for the new-look squad's unofficial unveiling.

There was considerable excitement after McKenzie won the final stage of the Tour Down Under in a sweltering Melbourne; however, it quickly evaporated. The launch and the whole concept of the team was a complete fiasco. The riders and staff numbered about 30, and they sat bewildered in a back room at the Cricketers Hotel on the A30 at Bagshot to be told by a frowning Sean Yates and Max Sciandri that they had discovered there was no deal with Jaguar, no deal with Jacob's Creek and the Linda McCartney money for 2001 had already been spent. Of Julian Clark, there was no sign.

Yates and Sciandri battled to save the team, trying to raise more funds and trying to organise the team on a reduced budget, but it was clear by the end of that awful day that there wasn't a budget shortfall, there was no budget. No money at all.

The riders drifted away in a sense of shock. Some had the good sense to hang on to the beautiful new Principia bikes they'd been given. Sciandri, picking up a ride on the Lampre squad, even rode his in the first Belgian classic, Het Volk, a couple of weeks later. The rest were left to seek their own fortune.

Bradley wasn't as devastated as some. For a start, he was within riding distance of home, unlike the Australian, Colombian, Czech and Spanish recruits. He was young, he was an Olympic medallist, and something would turn up. What turned up were the willing open arms of Team GB. In a brilliant move, they immediately put him back on the elite performance plan and reinstated his salary. He had given his country a medal and they'd not forgotten him.

Welcome home, Brad.

Rouen–Saint Quentin, 196.5km
Thursday, 5 July 2012

It's not exactly the infamous clear-the-air meeting during which sporting teams have to sort out their differences, but Team Sky do have a discussion about tactics before Stage 5 of the Tour de France. Another flat, fast stage designed for the sprinters spells more danger in the shape of crashes and another flat, fast stage designed for sprinters spells another opportunity for Mark Cavendish to win. How to combat these twin issues?

Sean Yates explains: 'The best way to stay out of trouble is to have your team around you and ride near the front. Also, the best way to win a sprint is to have your team take you to the front of the race. We feel that by riding more aggressively than we have this week up to now, we can achieve both our goals: keep Brad out of trouble and set Cav up for the win.'

Mark Cavendish is patched up and wearing fresh kit after yesterday's unscheduled bike rider/asphalt interface. 'Cav may have a little prob with his hand, otherwise ok,' texts Yates before the teams roll out of Rouen for another nervous 200km.

While RadioShack-Nissan are doing what they have done effectively all week in controlling the race for the yellow jersey and making sure the break doesn't disappear into the distance and ruin things, this time Team Sky are in closer attendance, especially in the last 50km as the pace rises and pulses follow the pace. All eight remaining members of the original nine-man team mass near the front, Wiggins enjoying the protection that a *grand patron* receives and Cavendish benefiting from a smooth ride to the business end of the race. The World Champion does indeed have a sore hand from yesterday's spill but he feels good enough to tell his teammates that he is ready to contest the shakedown in Saint Quentin.

Peta Todd is not called upon to express her frustrations when the inevitable big smackdown comes, this time with only 3km remaining. That's because the new team tactic has come up trumps and the squad's position at the head of the fast-travelling peloton has kept them out of the carnage for once. If only they'd listened to her earlier. The green jersey of Peter Sagan is not so fortunate; his scrapes mirror Cavendish's rapidly healing contusions. His girlfriend's thoughts remain her own.

The usual suspects jockey and harry each other for their sprinting positions. Cavendish, having been close to the front, drops back, expecting the winning sprint to be a late one due to the draggy uphill finish and the possibility of some cross-winds. The World Champion doesn't make a lot of mistakes, but this is definitely one of them, as he leaves himself too much ground to make up in the final 300m. Matt Goss is the first to break cover and he opens up a gap on the others, but he has made the opposite mistake to Cavendish and has gone too early. The cannier Greipel – who else? – has timed his run to perfection. Today he is able to swat away criticism that a crash has gifted him the stage as he has proved himself a worthy winner over the best sprinters in the race. Only Sagan and Tyler Farrar are missing from the vanquished; the American being restrained by his team from entering the Argos-Shimano bus after the event to launch a right hook at Tom Veelers, the perceived architect of his misfortune. Dave Brailsford's earlier observation that 'sprinters crash' probably wouldn't have gone down too well with Farrar at that precise moment. Emotions were riding high.

Cavendish decently declined to blame his injuries for missing out on win number 22. Greipel's second stage win and Sagan's absence from the top places has tightened up the battle for the green jersey, with Cav in fourth spot behind a closely grouped Sagan, Goss and Greipel.

Perhaps Team Sky's new-found aggression and cohesion will deliver the twin prizes of yellow and green after all?

Objective 1 has certainly been achieved today, with no members of the squad suffering mishaps and Wiggins's second place overall comfortably conserved again. The first mountains of the Tour are looming on the horizon, and Cancellara has publicly admitted that his tenure in yellow is unlikely to survive the first big obstacle, La Planche des Belle Filles in two days' time. The Vosges mountains are outgunned by the Alps and Pyrenees, but have some very difficult slopes to trouble the best riders, and most teams have taken the trouble to recce Saturday's stage finish. If all the favourites for overall victory in this race stay together and Cancellara drops away on the struggle up to the finish at 'Pretty Girls Plain' then we will see Bradley Wiggins of Great Britain pull on a Tour de France yellow jersey for the very first time.

Objective 2 has been a qualified success, with a display of team unity and brotherhood delivering Mark Cavendish to the finishing kick in fine position, but the Manx rider was unable to convert the approach with a victory. Tomorrow will be the last chance for sprinters to shine for a little while. We can expect him to be keen to show Greipel who is the boss.

MATT ILLINGWORTH WAS A bloody good bike rider. A talented time triallist from Westcliff-on-Sea in Essex ('Don't put Southend'), the tall cyclist was in great demand for teams on the British road circuit as the powerful horse who could drag races back together for faster-finishing teammates.

He rode for such teams as GS Strada, Kodak, Brite and Linda McCartney in a ten-year career upon the roads of Great Britain and the tracks of the world. He won two medals on the velodrome at the Commonwealth Games in Kuala Lumpur and that's where he first got to know Bradley Wiggins properly.

'I'd seen the skinny kid at a few races and I knew he was pretty good. His legs looked too long for his body. The longer socks were starting to get fashionable then – George Hincapie was wearing them – and there was a big debate about whether they were cool or not. They were made for Brad. He wore them so long you could have easily got shin pads in them, as was pointed out more than once in the bunch.'

Wiggins was drafted into Illingworth's England team pursuit squad for the Commonwealth Games. He made an immediate impression on the older rider, one that developed into a friendship that endures today, despite Illingworth emigrating to Australia in the early part of this century.

'The thing I remember most about Kuala Lumpur was Brad wiping his arse on a bit of paper and shoving it down the back of the fridge at the place we were staying at. After a week the smell was atrocious. Colin Sturgess eventually found it, pulled it out and went mental. "Who the fuck would be such a dirty bastard?" he was screaming. This weedy eighteen-year old, who had hardly said a word the whole trip, just looked at Sturge completely deadpan and went: 'It was Illingworth.' Thanks to his almost monkish silence up to that point, they believed him, too. I liked him a lot.'

Being cool was always as important as being good for Brad, even in those days.

'We were going for training rides in Malaysia, and it was, like, I don't know, 40 degrees or something and 98% humidity. Mental. We were ripping the arms off our training kit and rolling up our shorts like Yates, blaming it on being too hot but really just trying to get a nice tan to take home to England. Brad would be there in legwarmers. 'Pros never train in shorts,' he said. He'd been watching old Tour de France videos and seeing Delgado and Indurain riding mountain time trial preps in thermal jackets and tights in July. You could see him thinking, "I want to be them." And now he is, really.'

Matt would be the first to admit that the general approach to racing was a bit less serious than nowadays, and he was one of the last of the old guard who could party hard and still race the next day. For a while Brad was happy to join their ranks.

'We were up in Edinburgh for a track meet as part of our World Championships preparation one year. The old outdoor track at Meadowbank was pretty grim at the best of times, and the weather forecast for the following day was appalling. Convincing ourselves in the nice warm and dry hotel that the card for tomorrow was bound to be rained off, we went on a massive bender. The next day, we woke up mid-morning with horrific hangovers and pulled back the curtains to piercing blue skies and searing sunshine. That was the worst day's racing I've ever got through, but we got through it.

'A bunch of us went out to watch the Ghent Six when Brad and Rob Hayles were riding, supposedly to support them. We must have embarrassed them horribly, hurling abuse at them for six whole days, especially during quiet periods in the racing. It's much more fun then. My season had ended and I was kicking back a bit . . . I won't go into detail, I look bad enough as it is.'

Wiggins's success has not come as a surprise to his old teammate.

'No, not at all. From day one he was different gravy. And he just loved it so much. He was a pleasure to be around. I know I'll be telling young kids in my shop in years to come about how I used to ride with Bradley Wiggins. Well, if I'm honest, I'm already doing it. And telling them how Sturge used to pull Brad's pants down when he wasn't looking.'

Illingworth had a great career that he can look back upon with pride: an Olympian, a Commonwealth Games medallist, a host of World Championship appearances and stage wins and podium places on the track and on the road all over the globe. Even now, though he may try to give the impression of being an old soak in an armchair, the antipodean Brit has a formidable record as an Ironman triathlete. But the buzz he gets out of seeing Bradley Wiggins bossing it at the Tour de France is as good as anything he got from his racing career.

'I get a bit emotional, to be honest. When you see him sweating up a big mountain, digging in and holding all those other guys who're trying to spit him out, and he's just saying to them, "I'm still here." In the time trials these days, he's unbelievable. So smooth, so powerful, it's a shock if he doesn't win. I've known him for such a long time, seen him grow from a boy into a man and become a global superstar, but he hasn't changed one bit. He's a bit of a geezer who happens to be the best bike rider in the world. And that's not a bad thing to be, is it?'

Épernay–Metz, 207.5km
Friday, 6 July 2012

Cadel Evans's triumph in becoming the first Australian Tour de France winner a year ago was all the more impressive for those he beat. The two dominant riders of recent tours are Andy Schleck and Alberto Contador, and Evans managed to put both to the sword.

Andy Schleck would have been favourite to win this new edition of the world's greatest bike race if he'd been here. The Luxembourger has a similar build to Bradley Wiggins: over six feet tall but slim enough to be described as painfully thin at anywhere but a bike race. He has reached Paris in second place three times, despite still being only 27. One of those results was upgraded to the status of champion after the winner was found to have cheated. More on that later . . .

Schleck has always been a popular rider, largely due to the attacking style that always sees him jumping up the road in the mountains. It's not just the mountains either: he won a memorable victory in the world's oldest classic, Liège–Bastogne–Liège by attacking early in the race and riding away from the strongest of fields. His relationship with his older brother Frank is also a fascination for fans, the two of them flanking Evans on the final podium in Paris last year. One school of thought says that the support the two men show each other adds up to a powerful weapon that is worth more than the sum of its parts. Others claim that Andy could make his big attacks stick a bit better if he wasn't so worried about dropping his brother along with his rivals.

One thing is certain about Andy Schleck: he is awful at time trialling. Needing to finish within 57 seconds of Cadel

Evans to secure victory at the 42km time trial that was the last stage before the procession along the Champs-Élysées, he contrived to lose a staggering two and a half minutes in less than an hour of racing. Given that the three attributes needed to win the Tour de France are habitually given as: a) ability to climb, b) ability to time trial, and c) ability to ride for three weeks without a bad day, it is astonishing to find a champion who is so poor at one of them. His great ability lies in the hills and people love him for his weaknesses as much as his strengths.

Ironically, it was time trialling problems that led to his disappointing non-appearance in this year's race. While Bradley Wiggins and Cadel Evans were honing their form for July by riding the Critérium du Dauphiné, Schleck was destroying his own by falling off in the same race. Clearly struggling with his time trial bike in the high winds, he got himself all mixed up in a corner as his disc wheel took a strong gust and control was lost. Though he was unhurt to the degree that he got up and hopped back on at the time, he was clearly in pain, and it was later revealed that he had fractured his pelvis in the spill and would be a non-starter. Frank Schleck would take up the family standard and lead the RadioShack-Nissan team into battle in his absence.

In each of his first two charges towards yellow, 2009 and 2010, Andy Schleck was up against another modern superstar, Alberto Contador. A glittering career has been dogged by accusations and revelations of doping that have reduced his reputation as one of the true greats to something closer to a pariah. The huge shame is, of course, that Contador's Tour wins of 2007 and 2009, and the title he was stripped of in 2010, were incredibly exciting races to watch – now forever devalued.

In 2007, the young Spaniard was following in the footsteps of the recently retired Discovery team leader, Lance Armstrong himself. Already tarred with the 'doper' brush after being implicated in the Spanish Operación Puerto (Operation Mountain Pass) drugs case that cast long shadows across all of cycling, Contador found himself cast as the good guy in the Tour as his rival for yellow Michael Rasmussen was thrown off the race. His relentless attacking and refusal to sit down for long in the mountains gained him many fans. At just 24, he was their future.

They were unable to see Contador defend his title the following year, when the Astana team he had joined after the closure of the Discovery squad were denied entry to the Tour de France due to, you've guessed it, previous cheating with performance-enhancing substances. Sitting on a beach after a successful spring 2008, he got a call to say he would be riding the Giro d'Italia, starting the following weekend. He turned up. He won. He went on to the Vuelta a España with a bit more preparation and won that too in short order.

His 2009 Tour de France plans were complicated by the appearance on his team of the comeback kid. Lance Armstrong, hugely influential at the Astana set-up now that it was run by his old backroom team, decided he still had a point to prove and would come out of retirement. The team went into the race with two leaders and a great deal of internal stress, but there was only one winner. Contador crushed the opposition outside and inside his team with some stunning attacks in the mountains. Armstrong was third with the emergent Andy Schleck splitting the Astana teammates.

The anticipated showdown between the newly established golden generation of Contador and Schleck raged across France in July 2010. Controversy fired the rivalry, when Contador attacked after Schleck had a mechanical problem on the Pyrenean giant, the Col du Tourmalet. That moment proved pivotal with Spain beating Luxembourg by 39 seconds – exactly the same amount of time Schleck had lost on that stage.

Bitterness turned to rancour and lengthy arguments when Contador was found to have the forbidden substance Clenbuterol in his system. The case dragged on for more than a year. Contador rode the 2011 Giro in case he was unable, as seemed likely, to be allowed to ride the Tour. He won the Giro at a canter, then gained entry to the Tour after all.

However, he wasn't the force he had been in previous years, either through lack of preparation or lack of illegal preparation, and he ceded control to Schleck and eventually Evans.

Andy Schleck was retrospectively awarded the 2010 race, but it wasn't the same as winning in Paris. And he will have to wait until 2013 at the earliest to try that again. So will Alberto Contador, sitting out 2012 to serve his long overdue ban and mourn the loss of many of his victories over the past two years.

It all meant that the way was clear for Bradley Wiggins to establish himself as the rightful successor to the Tour de France throne. The order was still a tall one: see off Cadel Evans, Vincenzo Nibali, Frank Schleck, Jurgen Van Den Broeck, Robert Gesink, Ryder Hesjedal, Denis Menchov, Alejandro Valverde and any number of day-to-day issues. But not Andy Schleck or Alberto Contador. Brad has 99 problems but the Schleck ain't one of them.

*

Today's run from Épernay to Metz is dead flat and the last chance for the fast men to flex their muscles before everything tilts upwards in the Vosges tomorrow. A nice steady day, perhaps, a good day for a break full of non-contenders to get away and give the peloton a day off from chasing and crashing.

I wouldn't bet on it.

There are as many incidents today as the rest of the week put together. André Greipel manages to hit the deck twice and dislocate his shoulder before the race gets anywhere near Metz. Things begin to break up, with small groups of fallers and those caught behind them chasing at various intervals back down the road. Race radio is struggling to keep up with the dozens of little accidents and a couple of big ones.

Team Sky are concentrating on yesterday's tactic of riding near the front but it's not easy. Lots of the spills are near the front. There are still 25km to go when the day's biggest quake hits, with a pile-up sending a shudder of aftershocks back through the bunch. Richie Porte is one of those to lose his wheels and pick up some scrapes and grazes in exchange. The main damage is in race terms rather than personal injury though, as a sizeable group is delayed behind the mess, just as the spearhead at the front of the race is driving at top speed to capture the day's break and set up the big sprint.

That big sprint doesn't include Mark Cavendish. The World Champion answers some of the critics of his bike handling as he uses all his teenage BMX nous to avoid the smash that happens right in front of him. Unfortunately, his desperate braking and skidding brings about a puncture instead of a shunt, and he is forced to wait like everybody else. Boasson Hagen is there too, slipping quietly out of the overall top ten with the delay.

Up the road in the front group, Bradley Wiggins and Cadel Evans would love the time to breathe a sigh of relief, but they're both flat out to hold their forward positions and avoid any more mess. Cancellara is there, too, his custody of the yellow jersey seemingly allowed to run its natural course and not be taken off him a day early by misfortune. He has worn it easily and proudly for a week now.

More amazingly, as the remaining contenders line up for the sprint, is the appearance in the Lotto Belisol train of André Greipel. 'I didn't want to sprint, but my teammates talked me into it,' explains the injured German later.

He won't be taking stage number 3 today, though. Stage number 3 is instead the reward for the incredible Peter Sagan, showing that he can outpace the fast men on the flat as well as the strong men on the tough finishes. That green jersey is starting to look very comfortable now.

Time to look back up the road and count the casualties rolling in. Those with pretensions of a decent finish in a couple of weeks' time include Frank Schleck, Dutch climber Robert Gesink, and Garmin-Sharp's Ryder Hesjedal, who loses a whopping thirteen minutes plus.

Two men who will need to steady their nerves this evening are Dave Brailsford and Sean Yates. 'Five minutes before that crash happened Brad came right up to the front with Christian [Knees] and it was one of the best moves he's made so far,' says Brailsford. 'The first phase of this race is now over and he's still upright on his bike, which was the main objective, and he hasn't lost any time.'

Yates had made a quick judgement call on Cavendish and decided not to call back teammates to assist the sprinter in his quest to regain the front. 'We found it quite hard to get towards Cav – as did the [neutral service] Mavic car – because of what had happened. We were completely blocked behind the crash and it meant he never really got any help.

'Bradley, Froomey, Bernie, Christian and Mick were all right towards the front and you saw once again how important that is. The worst stages are over now in that respect though and we're looking in relatively good shape.'

BRADLEY WIGGINS LOVED BEING back on Team GB. After 2001 had started in such inauspicious fashion, he was riding like a demon all over the continent, attracting admiring glances from more professional teams.

He even went to the World Track Championships in Antwerp with a broken wrist after a training spill and performed with credit in the individual pursuit, though not to his full potential, which was understandable with the injury. He managed to persuade the management to allow him to keep his place in the team pursuit side and was rewarded with a silver medal.

A second attempt at professional road cycling awaited after the abortive Linda McCartney rocket had stalled on the launchpad. He would be heading back to France in the Fiesta again, but this time it would be for Nantes, not so far away as Toulouse, and a spot on the well-established Française des Jeux squad.

The team was fronted by Bradley McGee, an Aussie who seemed to be the perfect role model for Wiggins. A great pursuiter and time triallist, he was enjoying a superb road career with FDJ, achieving Tour de France stage wins and lots of positive publicity for his sponsor. The year 2002 was Commonwealth Games year, and the two men would be expected to meet in the individual pursuit in Manchester.

It didn't quite work out like that. The 2002 season was not going to be one to remember for Bradley Wiggins. Keen to impress his new team management and fellow riders, he overtrained in the winter after his wrist injury and arrived in France exhausted and prone to illness. He struggled through lonely days in dreary Nantes and hard races that saw him shelled early and struggling to finish in outposts of French cycling. He was missing the good life of Team GB and, to add to his misery, was a lot worse off financially, struggling to get by on a first-year pro's meagre salary after the comfort of living at home on Lottery funding.

But that wasn't the worst thing about 2002. Brad developed an irrational sense of inferiority concerning his Australian teammate and namesake Brad McGee that completely disrupted what was becoming a good preparation for the Commonwealth Games. Despite his poor spring, Wiggins was coming into form at just the right time. His team's participation at the Tour de France – Brad had unsurprisingly failed to make the team – had left him free to train to his own metronome in July and he arrived in Manchester in great shape. If only his mind could be told to follow his body.

Terminally psyched out by McGee, Wiggins slumped alarmingly in the final after a great qualifying run and found himself humiliatingly caught by the Australian. There was no outward sign of disagreement between the pair of Brads at any time – Wiggins has often said that McGee is a thoroughly decent guy and a great bike rider – just this sense on Wiggins's part that he couldn't beat him. The disappointment of Manchester was replicated at the Worlds in Copenhagen, where his FDJ teammate's presence loomed large over him once more.

Things weren't going well. FDJ had lost interest in their investment – if they'd ever shown any in the first place – and Great Britain's greatest track talent was in danger of spiralling away from his goals of World and Olympic glory just when he should have been reaching greater heights.

Brad was called to a crisis meeting with Peter Keen, Dave Brailsford and Simon Jones. Reminding them all unintentionally that he was still a callow 22-year-old, Wiggins blew his top, suggesting that his medal haul was pretty good, thank you very much, and they should be grateful for what he'd done; not so critical. And it was his ball and he was taking it home. The quartet looked at each other for a few minutes as the dust settled, then began calmly to map a way out of the woods. Before he knew it, Brad was part of the solution and no longer part of the problem. He found himself signing up to a new credo that had one intention: making him Olympic Individual Pursuit Champion at the Athens Olympics, which were now less than two years away.

The main plank of this ambitious plan was the newly retired maestro, Chris Boardman. Ten years after his own Olympic success had inspired the new Wiggins, The Professor was hired to mentor his protégé to success in Athens.

If Brad had expected a few cosy phone calls and the odd chat on a long ride, though, he was mistaken. Boardman brought his single-minded scientific approach along with him and spent all day every day working on or with his charge, notating every training ride, every race performance and, most of all, every conversation. Boardman was a man on a mission and was going to be on Wiggins's case every minute of every day until the destiny of that gold medal was decided. A montage scene of Brad as Rocky Balboa punching huge haunches of meat while Chris Boardman in the Burgess Meredith role looks on holding a stopwatch and urging more and more effort is irresistible.

Brad had somebody else in his corner, too. He'd met Cath after the Commonwealth Games, a Lancashire girl who'd been around cycling all her life. They'd known each other through association on various junior squads for a few years, but now the two of them were in love and by the end of 2002 they were living together. Brad shelved plans to return to his miserable French existence and spent his second year with FDJ commuting to races from Manchester while Cath finished her degree. Just like his explosive arrival on the world track scene, when it came to girls it looked like Brad had managed to get it right first time.

The year 2003 was immediately better without being easier. British bike fans had something to cheer about at the classics for the first time since Sean Yates's retirement some years previously, when Brad made storming albeit brief appearances at the front of the Tour of Flanders and the outrageous cobbles of the Arenberg forest in Paris–Roubaix. From the northern greyness he headed south for the colour of the Giro d'Italia and his first grand tour. It was all part of Boardman's plan for Olympic domination and FDJ were only too happy to have their second-year pro bolster the team. French teams are notoriously disinterested in the Tour of Italy, so getting a spot was no scramble. Wiggins hauled himself over more mountains and was pleased with his performance over the three weeks. It ended a little disappointingly when he was part of a large group eliminated for finishing marginally outside the time limit on the last big mountain stage. The organisers were expected to allow them to continue but chose not to; it is their right, but not the tradition. The eighteen stages Wiggins had completed would be a source of strength over the rest of the year.

Given time off from FDJ, as he was not part of their Tour de France plans, Wiggins trained like a demon for seven weeks then travelled with Team GB to Stuttgart for the World Track Championships in great form and full of confidence. There was no Brad McGee to worry about this time; a strong Tour de

France for the FDJ leader had turned a little sour afterwards as he was tired and fell ill, missing the chance to take on Wiggins in the pursuit.

With no nemesis in his path, Bradley Wiggins cruised to his first senior title – Individual Pursuit World Champion. Bursting with pride in his new rainbow jersey, the new champ would be forgiven for wondering on the victory podium in Stuttgart how many races he would be able to wear it in, such is the pro roadman's dearth of opportunities to ride pursuits.

There was a slight dip in the high the following day when the Australian team pursuit quartet, who'd already beaten a confident England in the previous summer's Commonwealth Games, hammered Team GB in the Worlds final, setting a new world record in the process.

Brad was delighted with his new-found status and got ready to celebrate in style. He had failed to take The Professor into account. Chris Boardman wanted to know where Wiggins would find the extra couple of seconds he might need to defeat McGee the next summer in Athens, and proceeded to harangue the new World Champion about it all the way back to Manchester. Cath was very protective of her man and hearing him moaning about Boardman's constant badgering was making her resent what she saw as bullying, but deep down they both knew that Brad just needed somebody to complain to. He knew that Boardman was right, and if he wanted to be Olympic Champion as well as World Champion, it would be with Boardman's help.

Part of that plan was to get out of Brad McGee's lengthening shadow and leave FDJ. Boardman was instrumental again, finding a ride for Bradley Wiggins at his old French team Crédit Agricole for Olympic year. Brad left FDJ the present of the Tour de l'Avenir prologue in his last race as their rider and headed back to England.

After a heavy winter of bike riding, partying and moving house, the new team and new programme felt disjointed to Brad and he contrived to suffer an awful spring. He was going nowhere on the bike, backwards on the track and Chris Boardman was pulling his hair out. Problems were beginning to mount, not least because there were other riders with a claim to the Olympic place that, as World Champion, Brad had assumed would be his. Paul Manning smashed him in a pursuit in Manchester. Rob Hayles posted the second fastest time in the world and took a brilliant silver medal in the Worlds. The Worlds were held early to avoid an Olympic clash and Brad was tactfully left out of the squad in an effort to find some form. The three-man push for the two places was thrown into further confusion when David Millar, the World Time Trial Champion, threw his hat into the ring for a place in the individual pursuit and began some testing to see where he stood against the other contenders. Pushed into riding a pursuit for his Team GB masters at the Manchester Velodrome, Brad performed disastrously and abandoned before half distance.

To top it all off, Brad McGee was in great form.

It looked like curtains for the prize that mattered most to Wiggins. He wasn't even going to get a chance. He wasn't even going to get on the plane to Greece.

The turning point in Brad's season came shortly after that unaccountably poor ride in Manchester. Three events in short succession forced him into contention and turned everything around.

First, Shane Sutton barked long and hard at all the other members of the selection committee something along the lines of the old form-is-temporary-class-is-permanent argument. Wiggins was their best chance of a medal no matter what anybody else was doing. He was outnumbered, but he can be a very persuasive man.

Second, Paul Manning did an amazing thing. He called the selection panel and told them he no longer wished to be considered for selection, as he felt Brad's chances were better than his own and he didn't want to stand in the way of Great Britain winning an Olympic gold. What a man. Nobody involved in that discussion, least of all Bradley Wiggins himself, will ever forget Manning's actions, especially as he had a realistic, if outside, chance of a medal.

Third, and altogether sleazier, David Millar was arrested in Biarritz and charged with doping. He confessed and told all, was stripped of his world title, given a ban from cycling and a lifetime ban from the Olympics.

The road was suddenly clear for Bradley Wiggins. It was back on. He struggled over the mountains with Crédit Agricole in the Tour de Suisse and found his legs beginning to come back. Slowly but steadily, he began to find his World Championship form of the previous year. Even Chris Boardman began to ease up on the nagging.

In Athens, Brad went into the competition unseeded as he had missed the Worlds earlier in the spring. It worked in his favour as he threw down the most incredible time of four minutes and fifteen seconds, a new Olympic record and the fastest time in the world since certain types of bikes had been banned for being 'unsporting' a few years earlier. It was a remarkable performance, two seconds quicker than McGee and Hayles, although both men turned in thoroughly decent rides. In the semi-final he held a little back, having the advantage of going last due to his incredible morning ride. He still managed to slip under McGee's ride by nearly a second. The two men would be riding against each other in the final of a major tournament again, but surely this time Wiggins could banish any negative thoughts.

Bradley sat at the doping control after his semi-final ride alongside Chris Hoy, who was there to be tested after storming to gold in the kilo. It says everything about the way Great Britain has come to dominate the recent Olympic track events that the IOC decided to remove one of Sir Chris's favourite events for London 2012, yet the great man found something else he could win instead. On that day, however, sitting beside Hoy who was flushed with his victory, Wiggins could not bring himself to even look at his teammate's medal. He wanted one of his own.

McGee. His old nemesis. Could he overcome those negative thoughts?

Oh yes, he could. Bradley Wiggins cruised to victory. Bradley McGee held him tight for the first 2,000m, but the second half of the race was a different story as Wiggins inexorably slipped further and further ahead of his old rival. Displaying all the Olympic spirit that great champions seem to muster at their worst moments, McGee was the first to congratulate the new champion.

'Representing Great Britain, Bradley Wiggins.' Just re-reading those words and hearing in your head that first restrained chord of the national anthem – will we ever tire of it?

Bradley Wiggins, individual pursuit Olympic gold medallist.

There was a silver in the team pursuit, too, then a brilliant bronze in the madison with Rob Hayles. Brad was the first British athlete since Mary Rand in Tokyo in 1964 to win three medals in a single Olympics. He was promptly awarded an OBE.

And just before the Games had begun, Cath had given him the news that he was to be a father.

Tomblaine–La Planche des Belles Filles, 199km

Saturday, 7 July 2012

Chris Froome first permeated the cycling public consciousness during the 2011 Vuelta a España. He and Bradley Wiggins rode brilliantly on the climbs to the Sierra Nevada and the ski station at La Covatilla to show themselves and Team Sky as the dominant force in a race short on favourites. The pair's power on the climbs and their similar looks – long, rangy riders with smooth, steady rhythms – made them an easily recognisable duo, and it looked for all the world as though Wiggins would become the first British winner of a grand tour.

The race's long time trial, approximately halfway through the mountainous three-week race, was the designated moment where Brad would ride into the leader's red jersey. However, not prepared for the altitude of the day's *parcours* and guilty of not judging his effort, Wiggins faded over the second half of the ride and missed his chance. The man who grasped the nettle without even realising it was available was a bemused Chris Froome, now leader of the Tour of Spain, the world's third biggest bike race.

Team Sky had a decision to make. What would the plan be now? Shane Sutton, Dave Brailsford's right-hand man, was hastily parachuted in to help the team's inexperienced DS, Steven de Jongh. Sutton was clear: it's all about Bradley.

The next day, another mountain top finish, was illuminated by the odd sight of the race's leader dragging an elite group to the finish while his team leader cruised along on his wheel. The Spanish press were outraged, declaiming Team

Sky's tactics as disrespectful to the illustrious history of their race. The team responded that they were following a plan that had always been in place, a plan that they felt was their best chance of winning the race. The day looked like a success: Froome's outstanding efforts saw him eventually dropped, the *domestique*-cum-leader-cum-*domestique* giving everything for Wiggins. The Anglo-African collapsed into his seat on the Team Sky bus at the finish at Montana Manzaneda safe in the knowledge that his work had put his more illustrious teammate back into the jersey he had worn that day.

Team Sky had made one miscalculation. The final week would see the race head up the Angliru, the Asturian mountain that boasted the tag of The Hardest Climb in Cycling. With some stretches reaching 24%, it's ridiculously steep for a major race. Too steep for Wiggins, it emerged, when, despite more selfless work from Froome, he lost more than the minute he held over Geox's Juan José Cobo and with it the race lead.

What now? Team Sky decided to go on the offensive with both riders. Perhaps, if they could put Cobo under pressure over the remaining days, one or other of them could isolate him and take the jersey back. Peña Cabarga, the last hilltop finish of the race, represented their only chance. It also happened to be in JJ Cobo's back yard, and the local boy could count on massive support, spilling over at times into vitriol at the British riders' nerve in trying to take their hero's glory.

Froome was phenomenal. He attacked; Cobo responded. He went again; Cobo caught him again. Cobo passed him and headed for the line. Froome caught him on the last corner, passed him and took the stage; but Cobo preserved his lead. Wiggins battled but failed to stay within touching distance of the two climbers.

It had been an incredible race. Two British riders stood upon the podium at the finish of a grand tour for the first time in history, but neither of them had won, despite each of them having held the leader's jersey during the last week. Great success or massive disappointment?

The post mortem was a difficult one for Team Sky. They had to learn from the experience. Had they made mistakes? Hindsight said that if they had thrown their support behind Froome after he originally took the lead, he would have kept it all the way to Madrid. However, it seemed disingenuous to blame management tactics. Wiggins was definitely the team's big hitter; he had a fourth place in the Tour de France under his belt, victory in that season's Dauphiné, and he was committed and rested after his early Tour exit. Froome, on the other hand, had emerged only as a useful *domestique* that season and had few laurel leaves topping his name on the list of races he'd ridden.

The discussions took place behind closed doors. What would happen if this situation were to repeat itself remained the secret of those who had contemplated it. One thing was clear: Chris Froome would not be underestimated by his team in the future. In the face of stiff opposition from teams searching for a potential Tour winner, Brailsford tied his newest star to a lucrative long-term contract.

Team Sky would head to the Tour de France with both men in their ranks.

★

Bradley Wiggins knows that 7 July 2012 may not be the day he wins the Tour de France, but it could easily be the day he loses it.

Two years ago, in his first Tour as leader and his first Tour at Team Sky, the first mountain stage was a massive disappointment for him. He couldn't stay on the wheels of the leaders and he would spend the rest of the race riding for as high a finish as possible rather than the yellow jersey. The intense heat and the intense pace as the select group of twenty or so men left Morzine in the Alps for the finish above at Avoriaz had proved too much. No amount of tactical skill or team support can help at moments like this; it's just the rider against the mountain. Against his competitors. Against the world.

This moment has many names. The crunch. When push comes to shove. When the needle hits the record. Showtime. Whatever you want to call it, Brad knows that it's coming, and it's coming today.

Team Sky, like most of the big squads, have already been to La Planche des Belles Filles to have a look. Not only the first important point of this year's Tour, it had never featured in the race before. There were no old-timers around to give their advice and reminisce about ancient ascents, where the moves would go, where to dig in. That was probably not such a bad thing in Sean Yates's case. He had famously given teammates in the Tour of Britain detailed advice about the steepest climb in the race – which gear to use, where to attack and so on – before it turned out to be a different route to the one he thought he remembered.

There's a more technical and professional approach these days for most teams, spearheaded by Team Sky's demands for every last scrap of advantage, the marginal gains Brailsford is so keen on. Rod Ellingworth, the team's race coach, is charged with preparing the team for key moments such as this, and he had led the earlier visit to the little-known road in the Vosges. Before today's stage, the team sit back in their Lay-Z-Boy chairs on the bus, listen to Ellingworth's instructions and watch his film of the road a little more intently than on previous days.

Today it is Team Sky's intention to take control of the race. On the understanding that Fabian Cancellara's hold on the yellow jersey is likely to end on the 13% ramps towards the top of the last climb to the line – he has admitted as much himself – then Bradley Wiggins should inherit it if all goes to plan. It is decided, therefore, that the team will ride as if already in possession of the golden fleece, as leaders protecting it rather than pretenders coveting it.

There are 190km to ride before the bottom of the climb is reached, with a pair of third category mountains to clear on the way. Team Sky ride at the head of the race all day, daring Brad's competition to challenge them. Christian Knees is in charge for the early part of the day, the thin, aptly named German's legs pumping smoothly on the front of the peloton for mile after mile. Team Sky, of course, have a plan for the ascent of La Planche des Belles Filles itself. Though it hasn't featured in the race before, amateur riders familiar with the hills of eastern France know it as the climax of the tough Trois Ballons sportive beloved of this region, and the Saturday throng is lined along the wooded verges long before the race arrives.

When it does, it is the Norwegian Champion's jersey of Edvald Boasson Hagen that leads the way, his broad frame shouldering up the centre of the road, leaving the entire field strung out in his wake. His effort is so intense that the field splits behind him and the breakaway riders that have been out in front since the outskirts of Tomblaine are swept up immediately. Behind, it is the turn of Lotto Belisol's leader Jurgen Van Den Broeck to get some bad luck, as the aggressive Belgian needs a bike change at the worst possible moment. He finds himself not only needing to chase but separated from the front of the race by the back half of the split peloton. He is the second overall challenger to have a bad day, as Ryder Hesjedal's problems from yesterday's crash have forced him out of the race for good. The third big name to get a kick in the teeth is Alejandro Valverde, an untimely puncture victim.

Boasson Hagen is 'puddin' da hoid on', as Cadel Evans's New York teammate George Hincapie would have it. But behind him, Richie Porte, Mick Rogers, Chris Froome and Bradley Wiggins are all cruising, a menacing sight for the other riders. For some team leaders they're not a sight at all, as Robert Gesink disappoints the Dutch who have wagered thousands of euros on him and drops away, as do Frank Schleck and Andreas Klöden. It is, indeed, showtime.

At the front, it's time to really stick the knife in. After Boasson Hagen's sustained power, Richie Porte cranks it up, then it's over to Chris Froome. The team's true climber takes up the lead for the steepest portions of the road. There are only a dozen or so riders left, and Evans is seriously exposed by his lack of teammates, especially compared to Team Sky's numbers. The defending champion responds to his difficulty with immense strength of character and launches his move. Wiggins stays calm, knowing that sudden accelerations are not his forte, and continues his high tempo ascent, while Froome covers the Australian's move. There are only yards left to the line, and as the road steepens for the last time, Evans falters and Froome takes full advantage, charging past him to snatch the biggest win of his career. Brad matches Evans pedal stroke for pedal stroke and crosses the line inseparable from the champion, two seconds behind the ecstatic Froome.

'It wasn't the plan to go for the stage, it was just keeping Brad up there,' grins a breathless Froome a few minutes later. 'I gave it a nudge and couldn't believe it when Cadel didn't follow my wheel. I'm speechless. That was a dream come true. I'm chuffed to bits.'

Evans is a gloomy figure in the face of Team Sky's dominance as he looks into the near future: 'We could have taken a more aggressive role in the race, but when you see Wiggins has three guys with him and I've got one, or I'm isolated already, what can you do? It showed the strength of their team.' It's not a bad day for Evans, however, as he surveys the damage behind and reasons that he'd lost time to nobody, unlike the vast majority of his competitors. He is full of praise for Froome, a figure he'd known little about before this season: 'Froome was incredible – he rode on the front for the last 3km or something and he was able to follow me and accelerate past me.'

A princely sideburned figure takes his helmet off in the background and breathes deep lungfuls of mountain air. The Tour de France's travelling city generates a huge amount of carbon monoxide through its thousands of vehicles and mobile generators, but it is unlikely that any air ever smelled sweeter. Bradley Wiggins had ridden like a true leader and a confident winner – a man here for one reason only and with a team powerful enough to carry him there. Bradley Wiggins is the new leader of the Tour de France.

'My priority was to watch Cadel because I knew I was going to take yellow,' said the Londoner, as composed and analytical as ever. 'It's fantastic. Froomey's taken the stage and is King of the Mountains, and I'm in yellow, so it was an incredible day.'

One of the few other Englishmen who knows what it's like to pull on the yellow jersey had a proud look on his face as he leaned back on his Jaguar and turned his face to the sun. 'We laid down the law today and proved that we are very, very strong,' said Sean Yates.

Chris Froome is welcomed on to the podium twice, first to accept the Champagne as stage winner and then to don the polka dot jersey of King of the Mountains. It is one of the rare moments in the modern history of this race when the best climber, as Froome has clearly demonstrated he is, gets to wear the jersey. The jersey is decided by collecting points for being first over the top of the hills and mountains that are scattered all over the second two weeks of this race, so it tends to be won by a rider who is low enough on overall consideration to be able to slip into breaks every day and hunt down those points. Riders with higher aspirations – in Froome's case, protecting his leader's shiny new yellow jersey – have to forego this prize.

Foregoing prizes is becoming a theme for Chris Froome.

Bradley Wiggins steps up like he's spent his life on that podium instead of spending his life waiting for this moment. The jersey is made for him. He kisses the podium girls with the relaxed confidence of a former lover. He shakes Bernard Hinault's hand as if he's saying goodbye after a day in the office and they'll see each other tomorrow. They probably will. And the day after that, too.

Wiggins, the prolific tweeter, summed up his day thus: 'Honoured to be in yellow made possible by an incredible group of guys, big thank you and huge congratulations to Mr Froome.'

THE AFTERMATH OF ATHENS was not a pretty thing for Bradley Wiggins. By his own admission, he hopped on to a carousel of celebratory dinners, public appearances and candle-burning that would stretch through the autumn of 2004, into the winter, over the festive period into the New Year and deep into 2005. The whole period was awash with alcohol and the bleariness of a hundred hangovers.

It started as soon as the Games were over – several post-event interviews in Athens were completed in a bit of a haze – and continued through the Tour of Britain. The race had an end-of-term party feel about it, as the reassembled British riders rode hard all day and partied hard all night, culminating in a couple of infamous nights that are still talked about with affection and disbelief on the circuit today. 'Do you remember that night in Newport? Now that was a night . . .' Et cetera.

Cath was pregnant and still working that winter. Brad put his bike in the garage and left it there, spending his days in the pub before getting home in time to cook his new wife – they had married in November – dinner, which would invariably be accompanied by a bottle of wine or two. Looking back later, he felt that he was entitled to enjoy his time in the sun after the amazing success of Athens, but his eternal approach of doing everything to the maximum also applied to enjoyment and he admits now that he 'lost the plot a bit'.

The period was also marred by depression, a strange sort of post-achievement lethargy that was hard to break. The money that Brad had vaguely expected to roll in for a triple gold medal winner failed to materialise and it began to dawn on him that he would have to work for the cash his family needed. He needed new goals. It was the perennial problem for those who achieve their lifetime goals at a young age, especially those who achieve them at 24: what will I do now?

He had signed an improved contract at Crédit Agricole, but he had been so poorly paid in 2004 that it was still something of an embarrassment. There were no endorsement packages for razors or breakfast cereal. When the bike finally came out of the garage, its owner was a stone overweight and going nowhere fast. His teeth grinding with resentment at the lack of interest his team were showing him and the low salary they felt he merited, he listlessly began racing again. Crédit Agricole had him in the frame for his first Tour de France, but he was doing little to merit those plans.

Everything changed forever in March. Ben Wiggins was born. The excited father, to his eternal annoyance, was racing and missed the moment. Rushing home, he got there too late. Never mind. It wasn't that moment itself that changed the world for Brad, but what it meant for the future. He suddenly saw with clarity that he was the spearhead of a unit now, the man that would have to provide for his family, the breadwinner, the focused professional. The dilettante he was in danger of becoming was banished. Only the best would do for his wife and his son.

The new attitude didn't come soon enough to earn him that ride at the 2005 Tour, but, working alongside Simon Jones and Team GB again, a crack at his first World Time Trial Championship was lined up for Madrid in September. He trained hard for an event that was new to him. As a pursuiter, he was strong in short time trials, but the whole tactical pacing of one's effort in the longer tests was a fresh skill to learn if he was going to excel at it, and we know what Brad is like when he has a new hobby. Fortunately, in this case, it was trying to win a world title, not drinking for England.

After an enjoyable feeling of being back on top of his game again, the resurgent Wiggins was seventh behind Mick Rogers at his first Worlds TT, a result he considers to actually be fourth, as three of those who finished above him have subsequently served bans for drug abuse.

The good second half of the season led to an offer from another French team, Cofidis. Not only did they intend to pay him a lot more money than Crédit Agricole were laying out, they showed an interest in Brad and his future plans that had been distinctly absent in his previous teams. And they promised him a start in the 2006 Tour de France. Another dream was about to be fulfilled.

The Melbourne Commonwealth Games and the Bordeaux World Track Championships were both scheduled for the spring, which isn't much use for Tour de France preparation, so the man who enjoys competing for his country so much had to forego the opportunity to add to his medal tally. It was a tough call to make, but the Tour was filling Brad's thoughts 24 hours a day. That meant a return to one of Brad's other vices – over-training. He believes that he was never above 90% in 2006 as a result, but it wasn't disastrous and he arrived in Strasbourg for the *Grand Depart* trying his best not to look overawed. The Tour is just so much bigger than everything else in the cycling world that it's hard to stay in touch with reality.

Things got off to a bad start.

On the eve of the race, the UCI received a list of bike riders implicated by Operación Puerto, a Spanish police investigation into Eufemiano Fuentes, a sports doctor who had clearly been supplying performance-enhancing drugs to many sports people for many years. Cycling took a lead and decided to expel anybody associated with Fuentes from the race before it had begun. The team managers were instructed to omit those riders from their teams and told they would not be permitted to replace them. Jan Ullrich and Ivan Basso, the favourites in the absence of the freshly retired Lance Armstrong, were among the thirteen men out on their ears in disgrace.

Still in shock, but glad that men he considered cheats would not be lining up against him, Bradley tackled the 7km prologue hoping to land a top ten finish. In the end he was a very respectable sixteenth and got down to the business of getting through his first Tour de France. To say he did so without any great difficulty would be belittling the nature of his struggle to stay involved in the racing every day, but he did so with no more difficulty than the other sufferers around him, eventually making it to Paris in 123rd position.

The 2006 Tour will forever be remembered for the Floyd Landis affair. After appearing the strongest rider for the first half of the race and cruising into the yellow jersey much like Wiggins went on to manage six years later, Landis suffered an appalling day on the Alpine stage to La Toussuire, losing eight minutes on the final climb to his GC rival Óscar Pereiro. The following day, Landis staged a comeback worthy of Lazarus, riding like a man possessed to take back nearly all of his lost time in one lone break over the mountains to Morzine. He duly pressed home his advantage and took the jersey back in the race's final time trial to be acclaimed as the winner in Paris, the eighth time in succession that an American rider had done so.

Landis's glory lasted 48 hours.

He had tested positive for synthetic testosterone after his heroic lone break. Not for the first time the cycling world had suffered a seismic moment and not for the first time it revolved around the Tour de France. Eight years on from the infamous Festina affair it seemed that nothing had been learned.

Bradley Wiggins, who had believed that the racing in 2006 was infinitely fairer than in 1998, was devastated. In *In Pursuit of Glory* he writes: "'You bastard Landis,' I thought. 'You have completely ruined my own small achievement of getting around the Tour de France and being a small part of cycling history. You and guys like you are pissing on my sport and my dreams. Why do guys like you keep cheating? How many of you are out there, taking the piss and getting away with it? There is me trailing home 131st and, for all I know, I might be a top 50 rider if we all started on a level playing field. Sod you all. You are a bunch of cheating bastards and I hope one day they catch the lot of you and ban you all for life. You can keep doing it your way and I will keep doing it mine. You won't ever change me, you sods. Bollocks to you all. At least I can look myself in the mirror.'"

Bradley's willingness to speak his mind to reporters meant that he began to be held up as a sort of crusader in the vanguard of the anti-drugs movement, a role with which he wasn't entirely comfortable. He felt that his own stance was straightforward and he was happy to espouse it, but he didn't want to be a spokesman for his generation.

His thoughts turned immediately to next year's Tour de France. Not only would he be a year stronger, a year wiser and a year better prepared, the Tour was scheduled to start in London. London!

With that on his mind, Brad went to the World Track Championships in Mallorca and returned with two world titles: World Individual Pursuit Champion and World Team Pursuit Champion. An amazing week.

★

After a wet and dreary start to summer, the sun picked the first weekend in July to shine. Millions of people lined the streets of London for Saturday's prologue and for Sunday's road stage down into the Garden of England and a finish in Canterbury. The British riders on the Tour were deliriously happy. They felt as though their time had arrived, and none more so than the boy who was brought up a couple of miles away in Paddington, Bradley Wiggins.

Brad's chances for the prologue had been talked up massively and he was enjoying the attention, without really thinking himself a likely winner. True, he had just pulled off probably the best result of his road career to date, the prologue of the Critérium du Dauphiné in the Tour's traditional last warm-up event, but he felt that Fabian Cancellara was ideally suited to the fast twisting corners of the Westminster course and he expected the Swiss's faster acceleration to make the difference between him and the rest of the field. So it proved, with Brad extremely pleased with fourth spot.

The crowds remained huge all the way down through Kent and the French press were full of the wondrous start in England when the Tour arrived there to start the business in earnest.

On the first Friday, the last day before the Alps, the Tour found itself starting in a small village by the name of Semur-en-Auxois, not far from Dijon in the heart of the country. There were about 200km to cover between there and the finishing town of Bourg-en-Bresse.

Brad soon found himself in a small break. With the mountains looming, the peloton were settling in for a long hard day and were happy to let the break push on. Surprisingly, Brad's comrades in the move seemed similarly inclined, and they fell away to leave the tall Englishman on his own at the front of affairs. It was Cath's birthday and, knowing she'd be certain to be watching on TV, he set about getting himself some airtime. A couple of hours later he was twenty minutes ahead of the field. The bunch started chasing, knowing what they had to do to bring the lone ranger back before the sprint, but they hadn't counted on Brad's engine running so smoothly. Normally, lone breakaways can be expected to tire after a long day in front, especially one as long as this. Nearly 200km on your own is epic in anybody's language. Still he pushed on, with the bunch nudging ever closer.

Brad maintains that he would have won that day if it hadn't been for the headwind that stopped him in his tracks as he swung into the last 25km to Bourg-en-Bresse. He began fighting the gear in a way that seemed completely alien to the smooth style he'd been displaying all day up to this point. At the 5km point, the race swooshed by, leaving him beaten but proud. And famous, too. Everybody applauded the brave Englishman and they eschewed a crack at the winner Tom

Boonen, to talk to him afterwards. Brad swears that he hadn't realised that the thirteenth of July was the anniversary of the great Tom Simpson's death, but the cycling press, knowing what an avid cycling historian Brad was, were sure he'd meant the move as a tribute.

Wiggins was enjoying this Tour. He was 'on it' and contributing to the racing. Against his own expectations he rode a dream long time trial in Albi to finish fifth behind Alexandre Vinokourov, a man who had been struggling with injury throughout the early part of the race. Brad was certain he'd been beaten by a cheat, and his righteous anger was proven to be justified two days later when the Kazakh rider and his team were thrown out after his positive test. His teammate Andrey Kashechkin also posted a dubious time quicker than Brad that day, so the Londoner has always considered himself as third fastest that day, only beaten by Cadel Evans and Andreas Klöden.

The last mountainous day on the Tour was a clamber up to the summit of the Col de l'Aubisque, the oldest mountain in the Tour, first included in 1910. Wiggins was in a foul mood on a hot day and was not amused when his team tried to bundle him into a car immediately after the stage was finished. What the hell was going on?

Cristian Moreni, an Italian with Cofidis and a friend of Brad's, had tested positive. The whole team was escorted to Pau police station and arrested. After questioning and extensive searches of the team vehicles and the team hotel had been carried out, Bradley and his teammates were freed but excluded from the race. Angry and ashamed at being part of such a farrago, Brad headed straight for Pau airport, pausing only to bundle all his Cofidis kit up and dump it into a nearby bin. 'I would have happily set fire to it,' he commented later.

Back in England, the fire still burned, but he was calmer. The best start to a Tour de France ever had turned to ashes for the whole race, but the personal hit of beginning in your own home town and then your own team being thrown off . . . it was a heavy burden for Bradley to bear.

He believed, ultimately, that these problems – Rabobank's Michael Rasmussen was also withdrawn while in the yellow jersey for lying to the doping testers – would strengthen the sport. The younger generation of riders had had enough of this way of racing and this way of living. They wanted to race clean, know that their competitors are clean, and stop creeping around like the secretive criminals their older colleagues had become.

It was a lesson that cycling was finding hard to learn.

Belfort–Porrentruy, 157.5km

Sunday, 8 July 2012

Thanks to Fabian Cancellara's occupancy of the yellow jersey, Team Sky have been able to concentrate on staying out of trouble for the first week of the Tour de France. All that is about to change as the responsibility of the lead becomes theirs.

With the bubbles from yesterday's Champagne dissipated and the backslapping over, thoughts turn to the job in hand. The brief is to protect and retain Bradley Wiggins's yellow jersey for two weeks while scaling the Alps and the Pyrenees, hold it through two long time trials and take it down the Champs-Élysées on Sunday, 22 July.

That means a couple of changes in job specification for some riders. Brad can ride much as he has the first week, with his cohort of Mick Rogers, Richie Porte and Chris Froome close at hand. Christian Knees will continue to tap out the rhythm at the front of the line. The remaining three of the reduced eight-man team have slightly readjusted targets for the moment.

Mark Cavendish's biggest personal goal for the coming weeks is the Olympic Road Race at 2012, coming up less than a week after the finish of this race in Paris. He believes the best way to prepare is to complete the Tour, while some of his rivals are talking of leaving the Tour early to rest and hone their form. However, they don't have Cav's incredible record on the Champs-Élysées, where he will be attempting to win for an unsurpassed fourth year in a row. In recent seasons, he has appeared to increase his finishing speed during the closing week, significant gaps opening between his backside and his sprinting rivals the longer the race has gone on. Although the first week has had some good moments, the World Champion feels that there is a lot more to be taken from this race, and his hand is feeling better by the day after his spill on Wednesday.

For the moment though, Cavendish is happy to adopt the unfamiliar role of *domestique*. Not for him the train of dogsbodies ready to jump to his every command. Instead, he'll spend long hot days toiling back up to his companions from the team Jaguar loaded up with cold bottles and energy food for everybody. We will get used to the ungainly sight of the rainbow jersey stuffed like a tourist's rucksack in support of the Team Sky effort.

And a *domestique* doesn't need a *domestique*, so Bernie Eisel is being reassigned to team duties. This will largely mean riding with Christian Knees. The two get along well, chatting in German when they're alone. The language of the squad is English, and the riders and staff all make an effort to talk in the most commonly held tongue. Indeed, you'd have to be a pretty special performer to get a ride on this outfit if you don't speak English, as communication is high on the list of Dave Brailsford's priorities for forging a winning unit. Eisel is talkative, always the one with the instructions on training rides, always the one who knows where the best cafés are, where to find the best cakes, the best coffee, the best way back. Knees maintains a poker face; on occasion one corner of his mouth quietly turning up into a small smile.

Edvald Boasson Hagen has rarely been out of the action in the first week. When one meets the Norwegian, it is like being introduced to a friendly, polite schoolboy. Fresh-faced, always smiling and gracious, he is very popular with the other riders and especially the team staff who always feel appreciated by him. It comes as something of a shock then to see him about his business at the front of a race, his broad shoulders seemingly transforming him from skinny boy to rugby wing. His personal targets were concentrated in the first week of the Tour, and the two stages he had picked out as possible glory points had seen him thwarted by a younger, stronger version of himself, the prodigious Peter Sagan. Still, a quick prologue, two second places and a huge job of teamwork in putting Wiggins in yellow all indicate a decent spell since the start.

Now, though, he will become Team Sky's go-to guy for the rest of the week. Need an extra injection of pace? Edvald's your man. Time to set a tempo on the mountain slopes? Start with Edvald. Does that break need to be reeled in now? Ask Edvald. Versatility is his strength.

There are no less than seven classified climbs to cover today. With only ten seconds separating Bradley Wiggins on the Classement Général from his nearest rival, the defending champion Cadel Evans, Team Sky will need all of their men to perform their duties with diligence and skill to avoid his stay in yellow being an extremely short one.

The first hour is crazy. With the German veteran Jens Voigt leading the way, riders are constantly shooting up the road. It's a fluid situation, with groups forming, splintering and being caught, and then new groups forming immediately. The first climb, a small one by the name of the Côte de Bondeval, comes after only 20km and has the immediate effect of causing a number of difficulties for those at the back. The outrageous pace at the other end of the peloton is taking its toll and it looks like the sprinters' *grupetto* of dropped riders will form very early indeed today. They will ride to assist each other, carefully calculating how fast they need to ride to stay within the time limit and avoid elimination. Greipel is there virtually from the off, and it's not long before his burgeoning group swallows up Cavendish and Eisel, the Team Sky riders finding the uphill pace way too hot.

Robert Gesink is also struggling. The Dutch climber, much fancied for great things in this race, is clearly bereft of his best form. One for Wiggins to write off, perhaps. One less danger to worry about.

There are problems of a different kind for Samuel Sanchez. It looks highly unlikely that the Olympic Champion will be able to defend the title he proudly won under the Great Wall of China, as he touches wheels with Alejandro Valverde and lands awkwardly right on the point of his collarbone, which unsurprisingly breaks. Hard lines for the popular Spaniard. The attritional nature of racing continues.

Wiggins and Yates had both stressed the importance of allowing the 'right' group to go. Team Sky's vigilance and high tempo stretches into the second hour of the race as they fight to contain the attacks, and we are halfway through this shorter stage before the race shape is settled. Voigt's group pushes for stage glory, while Team Sky attempt to keep the lid on everyone else.

As the race heads over the border into Switzerland, the lurid jerseys of Liquigas-Cannondale are prominent at the head of the peloton. Despite there being a dozen or so riders a couple of minutes further up the road, the real race is here. It's clear that Vincenzo Nibali and his team intend to test Wiggins and put him under a bit of pressure. Though the race has seven climbs, there is a drop of 10km from the top of the last one to the finish in Porrentruy, so it's not as dangerous as it could be for Wiggins. He can afford to lose a second or two to an attack at the top of the final climb, the first category Col de la Croix, in the knowledge that he'll have ample opportunity to bring the race back together, rather than the all-or-nothing nature of yesterday's finish.

One man with a point to prove and desperate to claw back some losses from yesterday is Jurgen Van Den Broeck. It is the Belgian who forces the issue on the Col de la Croix, and suddenly there is a group of less than a dozen riders with daylight on the main peloton. Van Den Broeck leads Nibali, Cadel Evans, Frank Schleck, Denis Menchov and the Team Sky pairing of Froome and Wiggins. Over the top of the climb, this select group are travelling at such intense speed they've swallowed up all of the riders who had been in front of them at the bottom. All that is except Thibaut Pinot, the youngest man in the race. If he can hold them off it will be the first French stage victory in their own race, and on a Sunday too, with millions lining the roads and watching on TV. But it looks very unlikely given the all-out combat behind him.

Van Den Broeck, Nibali and Evans all try to force the issue on the run down to the finish, but Wiggins is calm, unflustered, confidence bolstered by having a teammate alongside him in the shape of the climbing genius, Froome.

Up ahead, Marc Madiot, former French favourite himself but now Pinot's DS at the Française des Jeux squad, is hanging out of the rear window of the team car and having what appears to be some kind of seizure. He is screaming at the youngster and hammering on the side of his car like Animal out of *The Muppets* shorn of his drumsticks. Thibaut Pinot responds and it becomes clear that he can hold on to his lead over the favourites for a famous victory.

Behind, Evans launches a move that can be described as surprise, shock or desperate depending on your point of view, but when you're only ten seconds off yellow in the rankings, nobody can deny that anything is worth a shot. Wiggins covers it smoothly and rolls over the finish line glued to the BMC team leader's wheel for the second day in succession, with Chris Froome in close attendance.

Pinot is already at the finish, being embraced by the man who has practically blown him home from his following car.

'It was a fantastic ride. It was a tough day and to do that last 10–15km into a headwind just showed how good he is,' says Bradley Wiggins of Pinot afterwards. The yellow jersey is still his, the ten-second lead over Evans painstakingly preserved by a big joint effort from Team Sky. He is typically phlegmatic when asked if the Australian's attempts to unseat him on a downhill and flat finish came as a surprise: 'I'm not surprised by anything in this Tour. You expect everything and then nothing comes as a surprise.'

Tomorrow is the second big staging post in this year's Tour de France: the first time trial. Just over 41km into

Besançon in the Alpine foothills, it promises to really set the field out.

Sean Yates, a former Tour de France time trial winner, becomes positively Zen-like when describing his approach to the next day's stage: 'It's the race of truth and the truth shall be told.'

◉

UK CYCLING COMMENTATOR ANTHONY McCrossan has been in and around the heart of the sport for years, from local races to national races, from the classics to the one-week stage races, all the way to the Tour de France.

The pleasure of listening to Anthony is that you never forget that he is, first and foremost, a fan. His enthusiasm undimmed after all the ups and downs he has seen unfold, it's at a zenith with the irresistible rise of a man he has watched develop from a skinny boy in Thames Valley road races into the yellow jersey of the Tour de France.

Asking Anthony to sum up his feelings about Bradley Wiggins with a few choice moments is like asking a child to choose their favourite bedtime story from a huge compendium. There are just too many good ones to choose from.

'Some moments are inspiring, some are frustrating, some are moments in time that make you proud and stick indelibly in your head. The thing about Brad is that, like me, like you, he's a fan. A bike fan turned champion. I marvel at him when he recounts which shoes certain riders in the 1980s and 1990s were wearing in a particular race. How he knows who won the Kellogg's Tour stage in Dundee 1988. He has lived and breathed cycling for so long, and he gets it.'

He winces when he thinks about the times he has been on the receiving end of Brad's mischievous London humour. 'There is no doubt that when interviewing Brad you need to think carefully about your questions. You need to think about what sort of response you might get, while considering the

Above: Bradley Wiggins aged two-and-a-half – with stabilisers. *John Taylor*

Left: Having watched her son create history in the Tour de France, Linda embraces Brad before his Olympic road race in 2012.

Above: With his father, Garry. *John Taylor*

Right: Brad's inspiration, Chris Boardman. *Getty Images*

Below: Racing, aged thirteen. *John Taylor*

Brad in action in the Individual Pursuit at the 2004 Olympic Games in Athens. *Getty Images*

Brad and Australian Bradley McGee congratulate each other after the Men's Individual Pursuit finals at the Athens velodrome during the 2004 Olympic Games, with Brad claiming the gold. *Getty Images*

Above: With his OBE in 2005. *Getty Images*

Right: Brad celebrates becoming World Champion after winning the Men's Individual Pursuit at the UCI Track Cycling World Championship in Mallorca in 2007. *Getty Images*

Below: Brad races past Big Ben in the Prologue of the Tour de France in 2007, the first time the Tour had started in London. *Getty Images*

Above: Ed Clancy, Paul Manning, Geraint Thomas and Bradley Wiggins in action in the Men's Team Pursuit at the 2008 Beijing Olympics. *Getty Images*

Below: Gold medallists at Beijing *(from left to right)* – Paul Manning, Ed Clancy, Geraint Thomas and Bradley Wiggins. *Getty Images*

Brad sets a new Olympic record while qualifying for the Men's Individual Pursuit at the Beijing Olympics in 2008. *Getty Images*

Above left: Leading the way against seven-time Tour de France winner Lance Armstrong during the seventeenth stage of the 2009 Tour. *Getty Images*

Right: Sporting the leader jersey, Brad is in relaxed mood before the fifth stage of the 2011 Critérium du Dauphiné. *Getty Images*

Below left: Brad celebrates winning the 2011 National Elite Road Race Championships. *Getty Images.*

Brad celebrates with teammates and members of Team Sky during his parade in front of the Arc de Triomphe at the end of the 2012 Tour de France. *Getty Images*

Focus of a champion: preparing for the Men's Individual Time Trial road cycling event at London 2012. *Getty Images*

On his way to another Olympic gold, Brad races through Surbiton during the Time Trial at the London 2012 Games. *Amy-Jane Cahalane*

Left: With Cath at the 2012 *GQ* Men of the Year Awards at the Royal Opera House, London, where Brad picked up a Lifetime Achievement award. *Getty Images*

Right: With Paul Weller at the secret Stone Roses Adidas Underground gig in London on 6 August 2012. *Getty Images*

Like father, like son. Brad is joined by Ben on the Champs-Élysées after his historic win in the Tour de France 2012.
Getty Images

Brad picks up the 2012 BBC Sports Personality of the Year Award, before being knighted in the New Year Honours list.

audience you have in front of you. On TV you can edit. In a live environment, what is said is what is remembered and you're at the mercy of your interviewee.

'Take my on-stage interview at the Braveheart charity dinner in Scotland in 2009. I knew Brad was in off-season mode; more fun and less inclined to give the pat answers you can sometimes get after a Tour stage, but also a bit more combustible. I thought long and hard about my opening question to him so as to get off to a good start.

'I decided to start off with, "I interviewed Alberto Contador in London a few weeks ago and he was complimentary about your fourth place in the Tour de France. What do you think to that?" Brad looked me in the eye and spoke confidently into the microphone I was holding under his nose: "He doesn't really think that, he thinks we are all cunts."'

In his earlier days as a pro, Anthony says that the World Champion pursuiter was unsurprisingly more in his element in the velodrome than out on the road. 'I remember Brad at the Ghent Six-Day, riding with a young Mark Cavendish. I went to their little cabin in the track centre and it struck me then that this is where Brad was at home. He knew the track, the boards, the racing. It was his domain. The crowd loved him. Now, of course, the British public consider him one of theirs, but then he was a Flemish Londoner to me.'

Anthony was sure that Bradley Wiggins could make a career on the road but, like most of us, saw him as a useful *rouleur* rather than a grand tour winner. 'For some reason, whenever I think about Brad's early road career I think about him in Cofidis kit. It must be that long lone breakaway in the Tour de France at Bourg-en-Bresse in 2007, 190km out front on his own. It was the fortieth anniversary of Tom Simpson's death and he decided to go out and ride alone all day, getting caught near the finish. It says everything about him to me: an individual with a strong sense of history of the sport and an incredible athlete who can ride for hours at a tempo to match the world's best.'

Anthony has watched a big sea-change in Brad since he joined Team Sky. Stories abound from that first season about his taciturn nature and unwillingness to give any more than was absolutely necessary of himself to press, media, fans or sponsors alike. Sometimes he gave less than was absolutely necessary. 'The press conference to announce him was, to be fair, a letdown. It seemed that Brad and Dave Brailsford didn't really know how to announce the biggest signing for Team Sky.' There was so much hype around the deal, which had been trailed for months, that it seemed there was little left to say when the move finally came off, and the protagonists were uncomfortable in that particular spotlight. There was more in the same vein to come at that first Sky Tour de France.

'Brad's efforts at the Tour in his first year at Sky left me frustrated. I wanted him to do what he'd done in the Tour the year before. But even as I stood at the team presentation at the start of the race, I already felt that his head wasn't right. During the race, he wouldn't talk to the press. He rode off quickly when approached, whereas all the other GC contenders stopped and gave you a few minutes of their time, even though they would probably rather be elsewhere. His aloof approach did him no favours.'

Anthony believes the aftermath of the failure to make an impact on the 2010 Tour de France was the turning point in Bradley discovering the lugubrious, relaxed character that has made him so popular today.

'I commentated on him winning the Dauphiné in 2011. He was incredible. I felt so good about his performance that I immediately put a bet on him to win the Tour de France. At the Tour presentation in the Vendée, I saw a different rider to 2010. He seemed assured, confident and this time he talked to the press in the engaging and humorous way that I remembered from earlier days. It made me confident that he had done his homework and was truly ready to be a champion. I looked forward to a return on my £5!'

It wasn't to be, of course, and Ladbrokes made a profit on Anthony's stake. 'We all know what happened and I was gutted, not just to lose a bet, but to see a rider in the jersey of National Champion of Great Britain crash and lose his dream. Or, at least, have to deal with the concept of paradise postponed.'

A conversation some time ago comes back to Anthony now and shines a little light on Wiggins's new-found ability to be himself and be a champion at the same time. 'It was at the Tour of Murcia. He gave me a bit of an insight into his psychology. He had got rid of his long hair, pretty much shaving his head. I commented on it and he replied, "You know me, Anthony, split personality. The one that enjoys life and the one, like now, that is in race mode." It seems to me that, three years on from that conversation, he has now dealt with that need to be two things and now grows his hair and the trademark sideburns. He knows who he is.'

When you've known somebody a long time, you don't necessarily want to talk about bike riding non-stop, even if it is at the heart of each of your professions. In spite of his love of the history of the sport, Brad in particular is well known for his interests outside bike racing. 'When I talk to Brad it's usually about scooters, his family, watches, old bike races . . .' observes Anthony. 'He can be great fun on a night out. He is an incredible impressionist. After Cav's win at the World Championships in Copenhagen, we sat outside a bar and Brad pulled off a few incredible impressions of people; so good that he could have been them.'

Arc-et-Senans–Besançon, Time Trial, 41.5km

Monday, 9 July 2012

As mentioned earlier, there are three prerequisites for any Tour de France winner: climbing prowess, time trial ability and the strength to perform for three weeks without faltering.

When Bradley Wiggins first became a professional cyclist, only one of those attributes was apparent. His background in track pursuiting was a typical grounding for a *rouleur*, the type of rider who can do a great job for a team, grinding out miles at an uncomfortably high speed and pulling a race along. They also make great time triallists.

The young professional's role models were two other members of that select band: Englishmen who had worn the yellow jersey in the Tour de France. Sean Yates, the great *rouleur* who went on to become Bradley's DS at Team Sky, and Chris Boardman, the über-technician who lifted science in cycling to an art form. Like Brad, both were Olympic pursuiters: Yates in the four-man team pursuit in Moscow as a twenty-year-old in 1980, Boardman the toast of the nation after his dismantling of Jens Lehmann in Barcelona in 1992. Brad first became an Olympic pursuiter in Sydney, winning a bronze medal as part of the team pursuit quartet.

The careers of Yates and Boardman took vastly differing routes to success.

Yates's path was the more traditional. Like the other precious few Brits who 'made it' in European cycling in the 1980s, he followed the path of earlier British pioneers like Brian Robinson and Tom Simpson in packing a bag and heading off to ride for a French amateur team in return for little more than a bed and a baguette a day. His appetite for work was soon recognised and he found himself turning professional in the iconic chequered jerseys of the venerable Peugeot team.

Chris Boardman was always a bit different; a bit special, you might say. He dominated British amateur cycling in the late 1980s and early 1990s, unbeatable in time trials and winning a lot of the road races he liked to enter occasionally. Along with his coach, Peter Keen, he revolutionised the slapdash approach to cycling that had prevailed until then. His stunning victory in Barcelona was achieved on a carbon monocoque bike designed by the errant genius, Mike Burrows, that paradoxically took something away from his athletic prowess, as Joe Public seemed to think the bike could have ridden itself to a gold medal. If they had been followers of Boardman's progress over preceding seasons, they would have reasoned that he would have taken the Olympic pursuit title on a Raleigh Chopper. Keen went on to become the trailblazing performance director for British Cycling, a role to be expanded and refined by his successor Dave Brailsford, now Wiggins's paymaster at Team Sky.

Boardman and Keen carefully stage-managed an attempt on cycling's Blue Riband, the World Hour Record. Taking to the wooden track in Bordeaux at the same time as the Tour de France was passing through the city, Boardman beat the record with a ride that catapulted him into the broader cycling world's public consciousness. Combined with his stellar amateur experience, the hour record enabled Boardman to pull off the unprecedented feat of turning professional as a team leader. He turned up at his first Tour de France in 1994 and won the prologue in the fastest time ever recorded for any stage in the famous old race.

It is unsurprising then that Wiggins's pedigree marked him out as a natural *rouleur* and 'tester', as British cyclists unerringly call time trial specialists. His long-limbed ranginess and smooth pedalling style, honed over many years on the track, were ideally suited to riding against the clock. He confirmed this as long ago as 2003, when he won the individual time trial in the Tour de l'Avenir, literally the Tour of the Future, the under-23 Tour de France.

His five previous Tour appearances had featured some notable time trial efforts, none more so than the near miss at the prologue in London in 2007, but no name-in-lights rides. But, of course, he had never ridden a time trial in the yellow jersey before.

Cadel Evans's 2011 Tour de France victory was founded on his time trialling prowess. Gutsily trading blows with the Schlecks, Contador et al in the mountains, it was the penultimate day's time trial that saw the BMC man shoulder his way past the younger Schleck and into yellow, the last time the jersey would change hands in that compelling race. Just ten seconds behind Wiggins on this Monday morning, Evans too could be forgiven for dreaming of wearing yellow again.

When our old friend Fabian Cancellara, serial World Time Trial Champion cruises through the finish line in Besançon, it is with the air of a professional confident about a job well done. Though he has dropped well out of contention for the overall victory after two days in the *moyenne montagnes,* he is still very much the main man in the time trial. This is his last chance to gauge his form before his next time trial, his defence of the Olympic title in London on the first day of next month. The Swiss Olympic team have even decided to take up residence in the Mitre Hotel for London 2012, situated on the race's start line at Hampton Court, such is their confidence in their leader.

'That should be enough to win it,' he reportedly tells his audience at the finish. Not renowned for bragging, we can accept his word that 52 minutes and 21 seconds is indeed pretty swift for the 41.5 rolling kilometres that separate Besançon from today's start house in Arc-et-Senans.

Chris Froome's time trialling career had inauspicious beginnings. Turning out for the country of his birth, Kenya, at the 2006 World Championships, he managed to ride down the start ramp and straight into a UCI official. It takes some doing to overcome a reputation like that, but in becoming a major tour contender in his own right, he was knocking out some startlingly good time trial rides, not least one at altitude in Spain last year when he took the red jersey of leader in the Vuelta. Today he flashes through the first time check as the fastest man on the road. Yes, quicker than Cancellara.

Evans is the penultimate man out on the course, and his time compared with Froome is amazing. Amazingly bad. He has somehow lost almost a minute to the Team Sky man, and Froome's leader hasn't even got to this point yet.

Wiggins is on his way, though. Watching Wiggins ride today is like watching a thoroughbred on Epsom Downs. Troy, Nijinsky or Frankel: little effort, minimum movement, maximum speed. Somewhere in a zone uninhabited by mere mortals, his stealthy black Pinarello is counterbalanced by the eye-catching yellow skinsuit of race leader, his mirrored helmet lens reflecting the road ahead as he eats it up. A single RAF roundel, the mark of the mod, sits subtly on the front of his helmet, Brad's sense of fashion confounding even the Tour's attempts to make him as garish as possible. Calf-high black aero overshoes mask the fact that the distance from Brad's knee to toe is as long as many people's entire inside leg. Those legs turn with a sublimely supple motion that brings to mind a Ferrari ticking over at 90mph in the inside lane.

He puts more than a minute into Cadel Evans in the first 16km.

Those first 16km are easily the defending champion's worst of the day, but there's no coming back from a deficit like that. By the time he reaches Besançon, Evans knows he is staring down both barrels. He has endured a couple of difficult days in the mountains, but his attacking performances have given him great heart and he has lost time to nobody. Here in the time trial, however, his traditional happy hunting ground, he is scrabbling in the dust left not only by Bradley Wiggins, but Chris Froome too. Tonight, sixth place will be his only consolation for his efforts on a hot day in the shadow of the Alps.

There is no discernible change in Wiggins's rhythm as he approaches the line, but with Yates talking to him via an earpiece for the whole ride and driving yards behind him in the team Jaguar, Brad certainly knows that he is 'on a ride'. Having the honour of starting last, as befits a yellow jersey wearer in a Tour time trial, he also has the comfort of knowing exactly what he has to do to overcome all those who started before him.

He breaks the beam at 51 minutes and 24 seconds, and wins his first ever stage in the Tour de France. There is something magnificent about yellow jersey wearers winning stages in the race, an affirmation that they are deserved and rightful torchbearers. Eddy Merckx, Bernard Hinault, Miguel Indurain, Lance Armstrong – memories of them popping Champagne corks on the victory podiums clad in the *maillot jaune* are powerful ones that resonate down through the years. To those images in our heads we can add Bradley Wiggins in Besançon.

While Wiggins's win is, to some extent, predictable – he is clearly in the form of his life and a master of this particular discipline – Chris Froome's second place is a fantastic bonus. Team Sky and British cycling in general can be forgiven for pinching themselves. Two British cyclists sit first and third in the standings of the Tour de France.

When Brailsford made his famously bold statement about winning the Tour with a British cyclist within five years of Team Sky's inception, it is unlikely that either of these men would be thought of as riders likely to fulfil that particular prophecy. One was a *rouleur* more suited to the cobbles of the north or the boards of a velodrome; the other was a virtually unknown African. It is to the eternal credit of both men that they were able to turn expectations upside down.

For once, they would even have a brief opportunity to savour their achievements, as tomorrow would be the first rest day of this race.

Cadel Evans splits the two on GC (General Classification), but he is nearly two minutes adrift of Wiggins now, and just a few seconds ahead of Froome.

'I'm just really pleased with how I put the day together. Mentally, too,' recounts the usually laconic winner at the finish. 'At the moment it's just relief and pride in myself for doing that.'

The key for Wiggins is that he has beaten the champion and affirmed his race lead. The time gaps and permutations of what happens next haven't yet filtered into his consciousness. 'When I get back tonight, that's when to start thinking about the context of how it fits into the whole Tour and everything. Numbers are being thrown around – you've got this on Cadel, this on him – but at the moment it's a lot to take in.'

Back inside mission command, the Big Black Bus, Wiggins considered his achievement and spoke to the Team Sky website: 'We're nine days into the Tour now and there were two tough stages before today. Everyone was tired last night and you never know how you're going to recover. Time trialling's what I do best, though. I get into my zone, know exactly the routine I have to go through during the stage and I felt great today. The minute I turned the first pedal stroke on the warm-up I felt fantastic so I knew I was on a good one.

'This is what we've trained for. Sean was saying to me on the radio in the last 10km, "Think of all those hours, all those sacrifices you've made." This is what that was all for and that really motivated me. All the hard work during the winter, missing my children's birthdays being on training camps and things. This is what it's all for. These moments.

'I didn't set out today for the stage win, it was a battle for the GC, but to get the stage win is a bonus and that's fantastic as well.'

BRADLEY WIGGINS WANTED TO get away from Cofidis after the Moreni affair. He needed somebody to be angry at, and it became the team. Though they weren't directly responsible for what had clearly been one old pro looking for a decent last payday's actions, he felt that the team were the first line of defence against cheats and should do more to stop riders cheating in Cofidis's name. He found an ally in Bob Stapleton, the man running the Team High Road project.

High Road was a very modern concept of a team. A holding company which was Stapleton's baby was set up to run a team on a certain budget. A sponsor would come in and foot that defined bill. The sponsor could change from one season to the next, but the nucleus of the organisation would remain the same. They had been operating in this way as the T-Mobile squad for some time, with Mark Cavendish making a name for himself as their exciting new sprinter. Unfortunately for Stapleton, the German backlash against doping, especially regarding the implication in Operación Puerto of the wunderkind Jan Ullrich, led to T-Mobile giving up on cycling and withdrawing at the end of the season. It was a test for the High Road business model, but Stapleton's approach was sound and the team would carry on as they had planned to in 2008, becoming known for that year's Tour de France by the name of their new sponsor, the outdoor clothing company Columbia.

The team were also happy to support Brad's ambitions on the track, an absolute prerequisite for any potential employer of Wiggins in Olympic year. While he didn't really want to race in the red of Cofidis again, a plan thrashed out with Shane Sutton and Simon Jones left him reluctantly agreeing that a late 2007 season of hard racing was the best start to his build-up for Beijing, now the only target that mattered to Wiggins. He was determined to go to China and come back with three medals, at least as good a haul as Athens, and perhaps he could even better his gold, silver and bronze from 2004.

In Brad's view, the big challenge was to compete at his peak in all three events, the individual pursuit, the team pursuit and the madison. He felt that the individual pursuit, being his performance alone and the first event of each Olympics he had competed in, had taken preference over the others at his previous championships and Olympics, and he wanted to correct that. He felt that he was the best pursuiter in the world; he believed the GB quartet ought to be the best team pursuit squad of all time; and he was excited about partnering his new teammate and Olympic newcomer Mark Cavendish in the madison.

To that end, Wiggins trained like a man possessed over the winter. He and Cavendish rode the Ghent Six together, the team pursuit squad put in some crunching training in Mallorca, and Brad himself put in long solo hours at Manchester Velodrome with the individual pursuit in his sights. The key stop on the road to Beijing was to be a similar one to the Athens build-up, the World Championships. This time round, however, they would assume a greater significance than a mere staging post and pointer to future success, they would be in his adopted home town of Manchester and would be a massive target in their own right. It was a great opportunity to test his ability to do the 'triple' of individual pursuit, team pursuit and madison.

The sixes hadn't gone particularly well for the new Wiggins–Cavendish pairing, but they weren't too worried. Cavendish was coming off the back of his breakthrough season, a long hard battle since early spring and was exhausted, just as Wiggins was running into the form of his life. They scraped a good ride in a World Cup meeting in the new Beijing velodrome to ensure qualification for later in the summer, then set their sights on Manchester as their real target.

The atmosphere at those Manchester Worlds was unbelievable. There was a feeling that Team GB were the real force in world track cycling now and they believed they could win titles in virtually every event, men's and women's.

The first part of Wiggins's own trilogy went extraordinarily well. Despite easing back in his qualifying round a little bit too much and finishing with the second fastest time, he easily dispatched the man who finished quicker than him, the

Dutchman Jenning Huizenga in the final to retain the title he had won in Mallorca a year previously. He was now a triple World Individual Pursuit Champion. As the celebrations and backslapping began, so did the real test. This time, he pulled away from enjoying his moment and deferred it until the meet was finished and the velodrome lights would be switched off in a few days' time. He believed that he and his team pursuit partners Ed Clancy, Paul Manning and Geraint Thomas could not only win the world title but break the world record in the process. He needed to prepare properly.

By the time he was back at the velodrome in the early morning light, he was totally in the zone, race face firmly affixed. As a result, he was able to commit himself to the team like never before. The racing began with a shock, as a powerful Denmark foursome blasted a super quick ride of 3'57". That would take some beating. The GB team knew they didn't have to beat that, they just had to be quick enough to make it to the final, where they believed that they could beat the Danes no matter how fast they went. They cruised round in the second fastest time to set up the big showdown. After a few hours, they were back at the track and ready, the febrile atmosphere reaching fever pitch with the local crowd high on success, excitement and plentiful beer.

It's unlikely that there has ever been a more precise display of team pursuiting than the one that Team GB delivered that night. The world title and a new world record of 3'56.322" confirmed their perfection and sent the arena into fits of ecstasy. Once again, Brad forced himself to turn his back on the celebrations and tiptoed into his room, where his roommate and madison partner Mark Cavendish was already softly snoring.

The crest of a wave that the Great Britain team had been riding throughout this meeting had not gone unnoticed by the competition. As well as those two pursuit golds, the team went on to win a scarcely believable nine world titles out of a possible eighteen on offer, the most dominant performance by a nation in modern history. The seven golds landed the previous year in Mallorca were improbably put in the shade, and all this in Olympic year.

No pressure for the madison duo, then. They were unsurprisingly marked tightly, and Brad was forced into putting everything into a massive chase to keep them on level terms. But all was well as he ground back up to the wheels of the leaders who had broken away and he handslung Cav into the action to win the points they needed. As so often at the finish of the madison, there was a little confusion as the judges checked the scores, but the Team GB management were in no doubt: Bradley Wiggins and Mark Cavendish were champions of the world.

The big night out deferred for the past two victories sprang into action, and three nights of carousing were crammed into one long Manchester night. Good times, and the Olympics to come.

★

There was no year-long bender after these championships. The quiet confidence of this crack Great Britain squad knew that Olympic medals were what mattered. Nobody wanted to miss this opportunity, possibly one never to be repeated. Surely, they wouldn't remain this dominant forever. Now was the time to claim their inheritance, stamp their mark on the Olympics and ensure they would never be forgotten.

Bradley Wiggins and Mark Cavendish both headed to the Giro d'Italia in the colours of Team High Road. Brad was delighted to have a spearhead in the team and relished the work of setting Cav up for the sprints. The new boy picked up two stages in his first grand tour, delighting his team and repaying his teammates for their hard work in delivering him to the line.

Cav was to go on to his first Tour de France, and Bradley was a little envious not to be supporting him, but his plan took him to the routine of velodrome and road training that he so appreciated. Routine had been what was missing in his earlier years as a professional, and he now had a much greater appreciation of what worked for him, largely through the efforts of Chris Boardman, Shane Sutton, Simon Jones and the whole Team GB set-up.

As he set about the business of 'getting the numbers up' Cav took an incredible four stages in his first Tour de France. In the space of a couple of weeks, he became one of the country's most successful ever Tour riders, all at the age of 23. Heady stuff for British cycling fans. With the blessing of Bob Stapleton and a huge pat on the back from his team, he left the race before the Alps to fine-tune his training for Beijing.

The Olympics were set to follow the same schedule as they were for Brad: individual pursuit, followed by team pursuit, ending with the madison. The Olympic qualifying was more comfortable than could be imagined, with rider after rider posting average times, and Brad found himself facing the unheralded Kiwi Hayden Roulston in the final. Unaccountably struck by nerves before the final, he sought the counsel of Steve Peters, the Team GB psychologist who had been an increasingly reassuring presence in Brad's preparation, despite his initial resistance to the idea. Peters reminded him of a theory that would later become a mantra for Dave Brailsford's Sky team: control the controllables. Don't worry about Roulston, you can't affect his ride. You know that you are a faster pursuiter than him. You know that all you have to do to beat him is execute your own plan, and you will be Olympic Champion. Again.

'Execute' is a great word to describe what Bradley Wiggins did in that final. He rode exactly as he had intended and extinguished any hopes that the hardy young New Zealander may have had of dethroning the king. It was another Olympic medal, his fifth, and a second gold. He was starting to be spoken of in the same terms as Steve Redgrave, one of his heroes. It was all a bit rarefied, and Brad tried to keep his head down as he had in Manchester and ready himself for the team event to follow.

Team GB cruised through the qualifying round, allowing Brad to recover a little from his three individual rides, then lopped a gobstopping whole second off their new world record in the semi-final. The others may as well have gone home.

Denmark were the opposition for the final, doing their best to avoid looking like the goat tied to the stake in *Jurassic Park*. Only the Team GB quartet themselves knew what they could do though, and they were only too keen to execute their plan. They took another two seconds off their own newly set world record to be crowned Olympic gold medallists.

World records aren't beaten as often as one might expect at Olympic Games, the recorded times of less importance than the glory of gold and winning a title. However, when an athlete, or in this case a team of athletes, have lifted an event to a whole new level of sublime achievement, world records are virtually inescapable. What a performance.

Now Bradley had to battle fatigue – he had pulled out six performances at these Games – to partner the new star of cycling, Mark Cavendish, in the madison. It didn't go to plan. Marked tightly again as in Manchester, a combination formed by the experienced Argentinian and Spanish pairs put the GB duo on the back foot. Once again, Wiggins was forced into a mighty chase, but this time a blend of fatigue and the determination of the other countries doomed it to failure. The dream team finished in the group a lap down on the medallists in ninth spot. Cavendish was almost alone in a devastating Team GB performance at the Games in leaving the velodrome without a medal, and was seemingly unhappy with what he perceived to be Wiggins's lacklustre performance. The ill feeling was not to linger, but it put something of a tarnish on an incredible performance by Great Britain. Somehow they had managed to bring home seven of the ten gold medals on offer in the velodrome, plus an incredible win by Nicole Cooke under the Great Wall of China in the women's road race. For his achievements, Brad would receive a CBE to supersede the OBE that Athens earned him.

Dave Brailsford had surely achieved all that he could in masterminding this unbelievable return, all under the banner of a drug-free culture and public money. Where could he go from here?

Mâcon–Bellegarde-sur-Valserine, 194.5km

Wednesday, 11 July 2012

The Tour de France start village is like a massive, moveable country town on market day. All the various farmers, producers, traders and hangers-on gather and business is talked. Or to be more accurate, business is hinted at and skirted round. A rider will chat to a journalist about how he is feeling, what he thinks the rest of the race holds, and where he hopes to be plying his trade next year, strictly off the record. An older rider will talk to a younger rider about the new team he's heading to and whether the younger man would like to join him there, strictly off the record. A younger rider will talk to a retired rider now in management about whether there might be room on his team next season, strictly off the record. A rider in his thirties will speak to an agent of his acquaintance about contract values and where he might be expected to get the best deal for the following year, strictly off the record.

But the real business is done on the rest day. These days, the Tour de France has two rest days, one more than in former times. It was one of the changes instituted in the wake of successive drug scandals in an effort to make the race more manageable without recourse to illegal assistance, along with a promise not to hold any more back-to-back 250km mountain stages with eight climbs a day and that kind of thing.

Most professional cycling teams follow a three-fold programme, meaning that they can have riders competing in up to three different events simultaneously. This means that there are few occasions when the entire hierarchy of the sport is gathered together at one time. When they do, it's more often than not at one of the large one-day classics that litter the spring and autumn calendars. There's little time to talk at these races as teams jet in, race and jet out again.

The Tour de France is therefore the most productive in terms of talking shops. The riders spend hours alongside each other every day, and though they're racing, there is often time for a few words between friends or for new faces to get to know each other. This will often develop into lifelong friendship, as in the early days of the Anglo revolution, when English speakers would seek each other out for a bit of company in an alien environment. Or even a long-held antipathy, like the one that defined the 'relationship' between peers Lance Armstrong and Robbie McEwen. Lance would allegedly make childish jokes about the Australian for the benefit of his many sycophantic followers, while McEwen would respond with equal maturity that the Texan should 'Shut yer mouth before I do it for yer'.

All sorts of banter goes on. But the real business is talked on the rest day. With all the riders, managers, agents and press gathered together in a surreal bubble that stays self-contained yet transports itself hundreds of kilometres daily, it is simply too good an opportunity to be missed.

The press pack on the Tour de France is well named. It can often resemble a pack of dogs scrabbling over scraps. Many of the writers here are freelance, travelling, eating and sleeping as cheaply as possible while desperately trying to pick up 'exclusives' to sell through their meticulously managed network of media outlets. No rumour is too outlandish, no rivalry too childish, no scandal too petty to report. In the face of such pressure, it's hardly surprising that so many riders stick to platitudes and clichés in their interviews.

On a ride with Team Sky in the spring, I found myself alongside the Spanish cobble specialist, Juan Antonio Flecha. For twenty minutes I tried to chat about cycling with him as he politely and not unkindly rebuffed my attempts to get him to open up with smiling monosyllabic answers and apologies for poor English. It was only when the subject turned to football and the forthcoming Champions League showdown between Chelsea and Barcelona that he sprang into life, speculating at length (and in word-perfect English) about the game, the coach Pep Guardiola's supposed move between the two clubs and what the future held for both teams. It was a fascinating insight, not just into the mind of a true Catalan football nut, but also into the defence mechanisms of a professional cyclist in today's media-driven goldfish bowl.

On the rest day following Bradley Wiggins's imperious time trial win in Besançon, Team Sky are the subject of three main topics of speculation. One might be forgiven for thinking that the talk would be about Brad's serene progression into the yellow jersey, however, the themes are: a) Chris Froome's supposed unhappiness at playing second fiddle to his leader, b) Mark Cavendish's supposed unhappiness at playing second fiddle to his leader, and c) Vincenzo Nibali declaring that he is not scared of Team Sky and will attack at every opportunity.

Needless to say, Chris Froome hasn't actually said that he is unhappy, any more than the World Champion has shouted his desire to leave from the rooftops, but it's something to write about. Nibali used his Liquigas-Cannondale team's obligatory rest day press conference to issue the perfunctory rallying cry in a perfectly normal way that became twisted into a perceived slight on Team Sky bullying tactics by the time it made it to the papers.

Elsewhere, Brad was photographed drinking coffee and reading *L'Équipe*. Frankly, they could have cut his head out and plonked it on to any other rest day photograph of any Tour leader over the past thirty years. Fortunately, he didn't succumb to the English cyclist's bane, the readily proffered bowler hat and umbrella as props for this picture. The man has his own style, thank you very much. As if those sideburns weren't enough to demonstrate that.

An old teammate of Brad's, former British Champion Matt Stephens, recalls his first rest day as a young rider on a stage race: 'It was the Milk Race. I can't remember where the rest day was, but I had it all planned out: a bit of shopping at the local mall, ten-pin bowling. Then the DS came in and said, "Right, get your kit on, we're going for a ride." A ride! I couldn't believe it.'

It's true. Those outside the sport are always perplexed by the idea of the rest day ride, and many inside it, too. Like 4,000km in three weeks isn't enough; they need to go for a spin on their day off. But it's an essential part of keeping the blood flowing, the legs turning, the muscles working. Team Sky and many of the other teams have taken this to the next logical level by encouraging their riders to warm down after stages, too, meaning that many post-race interviews are now conducted while the stars turn the pedals on static trainers underneath an awning attached to the team bus.

Rolling out of Mâcon the following morning, the remaining members of the peloton are actually glad of those few gentle miles around the town the day before. There is a feeling of solidity around the race now that the first act has unfolded and the French have managed to plant a flag in home soil with Thibaut Pinot's weekend win. There are also fewer riders choking up the road: Tony Martin has flown home to let his broken wrist heal up before the Olympic Time Trial, one of 23 riders who began the prologue the weekend before last who are no longer with us as we hit the halfway point between Liège and Paris. Perhaps today will be the day when the crashes finally relent and this race settles down at last.

Today's breakaway group is a large one, with perennial escape-junkies like Thomas Voeckler, Jens Voigt and David Millar swelling the numbers. Intriguingly, Liquigas-Cannondale wunderkind Peter Sagan has snuck into it, too. It's unlikely that his partners in the enterprise will want to tow him to the finish just to see him trample them in a sprint, so they will go hell for leather over the climbs to try and unhitch the beefy Slovakian.

That's exactly what happens over the day's biggest climb, the testing 17km Col du Grand Colombier. Wiggins is unsurprisingly coming under some pressure of his own, but he is comfortable with Edvald Boasson Hagen and Richie Porte marshalling the race and Chris Froome, as ever, riding shotgun. Two men in the top three is an intimidating sight for Team Sky's rivals, especially when they're surrounded by such competent support. Nevertheless, Vincenzo Nibali is true to his word and launches his much trailed attack as the race passes over the top of the climb.

It's here that Liquigas-Cannondale's plan starts to take shape. As their leader distances the peloton on the narrow, twisting descent using a lot of skill and even more nerve, he is closing on his teammate, Sagan, dropped from the lead group. On the flat, with Nibali's lead over the yellow jersey group reaching around a minute, they're a fearsome duo and they set about their work in earnest.

Sean Yates sends the word forward to his troops: don't panic. The Team Sky mantra has served them well and will continue to do so. The men in black, white and blue settled into a steady pursuit of the elusive Italian and his powerful lieutenant. If the shape of the stage had been like Sunday's into Porrentruy, Liquigas-Cannondale would have really had Team Sky on the ropes. But Yates, Rogers and Wiggins were all aware that not only was it further to the finish from the big climb than Sunday, there was another shorter hill punctuating the route. This hill, the Col de Richemond, proved to be Nibali's Calvary, as his bigger teammate faltered on the slopes and Team Sky reeled them in. A scare for the jersey, but no more than that, and all dealt with smoothly and capably by Brad and his boys.

Thomas Voeckler is France's most popular cyclist. Two long spells in the yellow jersey – the first as an unheard-of rider in Armstrong's long shadow, the second just last year – propelled him into public sight, but it is his do-or-die commitment that has given him a slot in their hearts. This year has been difficult for him, with tendonitis putting his Tour place in jeopardy right up to Liège and his Europcar team coming under scrutiny from the doping enforcement agencies. Today is the day he puts that in the shade with a ride of incredible persistence, attacking again and again, receiving no hope from his breakaway companions. They're all dangerous riders, men like Michele Scarponi, Luis Leon Sanchez and Jens Voigt, and all capable of taking the stage for themselves. Just when it looks like Voeckler has punched himself out of contention, he finds the resilience to go again, catching Jens Voigt on the long drag to the finish, resisting all other attempts to better him, and using his ungainly style to grapple a huge gear all the way to the line. France is in raptures: two out of the last three stages, their hero a winner again, and now the wearer of the polka dot jersey of *meilleur grimpeur*, too.

Wiggins reveals just how far the team is prepared to go to ensure the don't-panic ethos is carried all the way to Paris: 'We were prepared to lose the jersey if need be to Scarponi who was the best placed up there. This is about being in yellow in Paris and if that means sacrificing the next days and keeping the boys back a bit . . .'

Nibali, Evans and Van Den Broeck are clearly the true danger men for Team Sky, even to the extent that they are prepared to let a Giro d'Italia podium finisher like Scarponi 'borrow' the jersey. 'We do have to gamble a little bit here and we can't just chase everything that moves,' explains the leader.

Wiggins has clearly got under the skin of his Liquigas-Cannondale rival Vincenzo Nibali. After chasing him down on the Col de Richemond, Wiggins tracked the Italian all the way to the finish line and shot him a glance as they crossed the finish line. After earlier telling the press that he was 'not impressed' by Wiggins, Nibali went further after his attempts to unseat the yellow jersey had come to naught in Bellegarde-sur-Valserine. 'When we crossed the line, Bradley turned and looked at me,' Nibali said. 'If he wants to be a great champion, he needs to have a bit of respect for his adversaries. Sometimes turning around and looking into your face is an insult.'

Team Sky will have to continue to use their judgement as to how much danger any move represents every day. Tomorrow will be a massive test for that: a mountain top finish in the high Alps. Can Bradley Wiggins demonstrate that his discomfort on stages like this has been consigned to the dustbin of history once and for all? If not, all the hard work carried out so far by Team Sky will be like so many flies crashing into windscreens.

The best laid plans of mice and men . . .

TO DESCRIBE BRADLEY WIGGINS's relationship with his father as complicated would be like saying that Ayrton Senna was good at driving. It's undoubtedly true, but only begins to scratch at the surface.

Garry Wiggins was trouble. Sometimes it surrounded him and followed him; often it was of his own creation. Being single-minded and resolute must have been admirable preconditions to leaving behind a provincial life in Morwell, Victoria, to ride a bike for a living in Europe. Less admirable was his willingness to leave behind a wife and a baby daughter to do so.

One wouldn't want to assume too much about a man's character by looking at his actions in isolation, but by leaving his new wife, Linda, and his son, Bradley, before the boy was two years old, Garry invites negative speculation. To discover that he went on to abandon a third wife, Fiona, and a third child, Madison, in Australia nearly twenty years later is a depressing confirmation that Bradley Wiggins's father was an irresolute, irresponsible man.

Some might argue that his attempts to reconcile with his estranged son in 1997 via a long-distance phone call represented a worthy attempt to put his past behind him and start afresh. Others would say that such an act was that of a selfish man who wanted a part of his biological offspring's success for himself, despite having had no influence whatsoever on his upbringing or having made any attempt to support him during those missing years. Whatever the motivation, Bradley decided to try to maintain a friendship of sorts with his father from that point on and to see if he could understand the man who had brought him into this world.

Bradley had not grown up in denial of his father. Linda had been careful not to let his opinion of his dad be clouded with prejudice. She had told him all about his dad's exciting and slightly misty career as a track rider in Belgium and Europe. He was aware of his father's exploits without ever taking a massive interest in cycling as a kid, and it was only now that he was beginning to appreciate what that lifestyle would have entailed.

The irregular distant friendship between two men generations and continents apart drifted along with occasional phone calls, Garry usually reminding his son how good a rider he had been and offering the occasional congratulations, as when Brad became World Junior Pursuit Champion a year or so after that first call. It was to be 1999 when the two would meet for the first time since a bizarre trip to London Zoo seventeen years earlier on his one and only visit to see his son after his break-up with Linda. Brad left a GB training camp in Australia to have lunch with his father and two half-sisters he had never met: Shannon, a little older than Brad and with a life of her own into which her father had also crashed, and Madison, the little girl Garry had fathered with his current partner, Fiona.

It must have been an unsettling encounter to say the least, a family group where nobody knows each other. Tensions were already running high between Garry and Shannon, largely because he had walked back into her life after twenty years and expected to give her away at her forthcoming wedding, something Shannon was understandably not keen on. Brad stayed detached, trying to take in this strange situation and figure out how to proceed.

When Brad decisively called his father a year later and offered to come and stay for a few weeks in advance of his pre-Olympic training camp, he didn't expect Garry's life to have changed as much as it had. The attempts at reconciliation with Shannon and himself had been during a good period of steady work and a committed relationship, but everything had begun to unravel shortly after that odd luncheon date.

Brad felt that he might regret never having taken the opportunity to get to know Garry better, and he certainly had a good snapshot of how life was in the Wiggins Senior household. It involved a lot of beer, a lot of self-pity, a lot of anger and not much else, unless somebody was foolish enough to get in his way. By the end of three weeks, the nineteen-year-old Wiggins had had a bellyful of the 48-year-old one. He maintained the distance that yawned between them despite his father's attempts to claim him as his son after all this time, and they parted on distant, if not hostile, terms.

Garry occasionally made it over to Europe for a look at his old stamping ground and on occasion caught up with Brad at the Ghent Six-Day race. He would invariably be holding court at a bar, fuelled with beer supplied by his son and surrounded by listeners only too happy to hear tales of his unsurpassable genius as a track rider and drink the beer he so generously gave out via his son's wallet. He would delight in telling them about Bradley's shortcomings as a cyclist and expound upon the reasons why he could never match his old dad's abilities.

It wasn't what you'd call your typical father-son relationship.

Brad was woken by a phone call in the early hours of a January morning in 2008. He had been training in Manchester as part of his Beijing preparations and so was sleeping in his own bed for once. He got out of bed leaving Cath sleeping, wondering who it could be. There had been drunken late-night calls from Garry in the past, but not for years. A chain of events and long-distance calls that night revealed a sad truth: Garry Wiggins was dead. The truth was hazy, but it appeared that he had been drinking at a house party and got into a fight with the host. He had left the party on his feet, but been found a little way off at the roadside a few hours later, dead from a blow to the head. Whether the injury had been sustained in the fight or when he fell was unclear, but those were the facts. He was just 55.

Bradley talked to Shannon and Garry's sister, Glenda, in Australia. He made plans to go out for the funeral but then changed his mind. It was time to put his father and their tentative steps towards reconciliation behind him. He should be concentrating on his own family – his lovely wife Cath, first child Ben and the recently arrived Isabella – none of whom Garry had ever met.

Two months later, Bradley dedicated his gold medal at the World Championship when partnering Mark Cavendish in the madison to his late father. For all his faults and all the pain he had been through and caused, Brad remembered that Garry had been a bloody good bike rider. There had been few better madison riders in his day. It seemed a fitting tribute to a man who had meant so little, yet strangely so much, to the new World Champion.

Albertville–La Toussuire, 148km
Thursday, 12 July 2012

Back in the mists of time, way back as far as the 1990s and even the 1980s, the cycling season went like this: spring classics, Vuelta, Giro, Tour, autumn classics, World Championships, Tour of Lombardy. That was it. No Tour Down Under. No Tour of California. None of that stuff. What's more, races used to be run in a logical start-slow-get-faster sort of way. When the Tour went through a French rider's home town, he had time to hop off and share a glass of bubbly at *un picnic en famille* before lolloping back up to join the leisurely peloton.

Then things began to change. People started putting up a bit more money for folks to win their bike race, or even just for them to come and ride it, especially if it was in some far flung place. The decidedly two-bit Tour de Langkawi in Malaysia, for instance, became the fourth richest race in the world for teams prepared to spend two weeks in February riding through a jungle. Now, the Tour of Qatar and the Tour of Turkey attract squads chasing early season euros and UCI points.

Ah, yes, UCI points. Points dished out for results at races, weighted according to the seriousness of the event. It's all a bit chicken-and-egg, but people started chasing UCI points around the same time as races got richer and quicker. A rider with points against his name can secure a team entry to the races they want to ride. It's made racing more competitive but flawed: Saxo Bank team manager Bjarne Riis recently pointed out that it's not easy to get a *domestique* to sacrifice his own ambitions for a team leader and then be told at the end of the year that he hasn't earned a contract for the following year because he hasn't accrued enough UCI points.

All these things meant that the traditional way of racing was impossible to sustain over the course of a season. It was just too hard to ride all of the races, especially to ride hard in all of the races. Something had to give.

The first thing to give was the Vuelta a España. Rooted to its spot in the annual calendar at the beginning of May, immediately after the cessation of the spring classics, the Tour of Spain suffered horribly through the new regime of hard riding for ten months of the year. Nobody was turning up. It was fast becoming a domestic race, and even the brightest Spanish stars were finding it hard to find room in their year to ride the Vuelta. Even the legends Pedro Delgado and Miguel Indurain began to duck it in order to better prepare for the Tour de France.

The solution was to fan the three grand tours out. The Giro d'Italia would be the first one of the year now, moving from its customary appointment in June to May. The Vuelta would be pushed back to September with the World Championships even later than that to bookend the season.

To start with, the move benefited the Giro and the Tour, not that the Tour needed any help, as it had long been becoming a gargantuan monolith that dominated the calendar more and more with every passing year. The Giro now became the place to be seen for the Tour riders in need of a hard race before July.

The Vuelta was quickly cast as the whipping boy of the whole arrangement, and the new arrangement didn't do the World Championships any favours either, pushing it to such a late point that many likely contenders had simply had enough racing by then and stayed at home.

Faced with this alarming erosion of the world's third biggest bike race, the organisers of the Vuelta hatched a cunning plan. They reasoned that what the cycling public wanted to see were mountain top finishes and plenty of them. They wanted to see the favourites scrapping with each other day in, day out. And they wanted the drama to go the distance of a three-week race.

So, they made some key changes. Out went super-long stages – the TV viewers only switch on for the last hour, anyway. In came short, sharp exciting *parcours* that invariably finished on top of a big hill, giving the attacking riders more chance of hurting the competition. They also introduced time bonuses for those finishes, giving an extra incentive for attacking your rivals at the end of each day. And out went long time trials, a move that had two benefits. Firstly, it tended to prolong the race's action right up to the final weekend as there were less long settled time gaps between the top riders on GC. Secondly, lots of time trialling kilometres in a race tended to promote and favour a more defensive style: build up your lead in the time trial then protect it in the mountains. (This final point was a theme that 2012 Tour de France viewers were beginning to suspect awaited them.)

As a result, their race was revitalised. Nobody was ever certain of victory until they'd breathed a huge sigh of relief in Madrid. Time bonuses and big climbs kept everybody guessing from the first stage until the last, and the lack of monster stages made it infinitely more attractive for riders to come and give it a nudge.

Lance Armstrong was one of the first to enjoy the new format. His 1998 appearance was the springboard for his comeback after testicular cancer and his fourth place was a major plank in convincing him that Tour de France glory was a possibility.

The Tour de France has belatedly begun to look at the Vuelta's advances. The Tour remains steeped in tradition, however, the numerous doping scandals that have battered the race's reputation for many years could not continue to be ignored. In the same year that Armstrong was reinventing himself in Spain, the race was brought to its knees by the revelation that a Festina team car carrying illicit supplies for its riders had been rumbled by French police. Expulsion, police raids and even jail for the many miscreants threatened the very fabric of the great event. Drug taking appeared to have reached its dark zenith, with many privately claiming that the race could not be completed without chemical assistance. Yet two years later, the Tour was still staging back-to-back Alpine stages containing 425km and seven enormous passes in an eye-watering display of endurance for the riders. The stages were won by Santiago Botero and Marco Pantani respectively, both riders with histories of drug abuse. The image of a shell-shocked and demoralised David Millar after these tortures was the first that sprang to this writer's mind when the British star confessed to taking illegal stimulants four years later.

Things are a little different in 2012. Not revolutionarily different, but a lesson has been learned from the Vuelta. This 148km stage to the ski-station at La Toussuire is the *étape reine* of this year's procession through the Alps. In the last century, this may have meant anything up to eight hours in the saddle, scaling any number of high passes. Claudio Chiappucci's legendary win over Miguel Indurain at Sestriere in 1992 took nearly eight hours – a lot longer for those in *l'autobus* – and went over five huge passes to cover a total of 254km. The day before was even longer, and the day after finished on Alpe d'Huez.

Today, the riders will head over the massive Col de Madeleine virtually from the start, then the graveyard of ambition that is the Col de la Croix de Fer, before tackling the brutish slopes to the finish at La Toussuire.

Last year, the Tour de France's most exciting stage was an eyebrow-raising dash of just 109km, over the Tour's favourite giant, the Col du Galibier, then finishing on top of Alpe d'Huez. Alberto Contador and Pierre Rolland traded blows all the way up the Alpe, while behind them Andy Schleck launched the sort of gut-wrenching attack that gets fans out of their seats and Cadel Evans's fatigue-busting pursuit ultimately won him the race.

Shorter stages suit the fans and riders alike. But will they suit Bradley Wiggins and his defence of the *maillot jaune*? On the one hand, he should be fresher and less susceptible to the attritional problems such long mountain stages bring, but attacks are all the more likely. Evans, Nibali, Van Den Broeck, Frank Schleck and Menchov are waiting like vultures for the first sign of weakness. Will Team Sky be able to fend them all off?

★

Albertville, host of the 1992 Winter Olympics. Not to be confused with Alphaville, shoulder-padded purveyors of the 1980s 'classic' 'Big In Japan'. I remember it well as the singer had acne scars of Steve Cram proportions, a horrendous quiff, make-up befitting a deluded transvestite and, unfortunately, looked like me, according to my schoolfriends.

How to put this? It's not a place I'd want to be stuck in, falling as it does into that category of Alpine towns most often described as 'unloved'. Apparently, the more colloquial 'shit-hole' is frowned upon.

Brad and his band of merry men don't get to see much of it. Within a few minutes they're already setting a frantic tempo on the Col de la Madeleine in an attempt to contain a furious breakaway group intent on landing a stage win. The relatively short distance of 148km leaves no room for pleasantries and the explosive attacks cause instant panic at the back of the bunch as the sprinters and *rouleurs* try to organise themselves to ensure they will finish within the time limit and not be eliminated. This is a job they wouldn't have expected to contemplate until much later in the day.

Twenty-eight riders is a big breakaway group, even if it doesn't include any obvious contenders for Wiggins's throne, and Team Sky send the Norwegian battering ram Edvald Boasson Hagen up to the nose of the peloton to control things. Incredibly, the one-man team rides on the front of the race pretty much without assistance for the thick end of 80km. It's not until the upper slopes of the Col du Glandon are reached that his team-mates Mick Rogers and Richie Porte take up the reins.

The Col du Glandon is not an easy climb, but it is largely a white-lines-down-the-middle kind of road. Today, we're not going to take the Tour organisers' favourite route of going over the Glandon and down to Le Bourg-d'Oisans before a sharp left up Alpe d'Huez. Instead, on top of the Col, we're going to swing left up the steeper and narrower Col de Croix de Fer. Perhaps it is the knowledge that this harder part is coming, perhaps he is nervous, or perhaps he just feels good. Whatever the reason, Cadel Evans's attack on the Glandon comes as a surprise. We're only halfway through the stage and Team Sky's Aussie duo are going pretty hard, but the defending champion shoots upwards from the group in search of the seconds he has ceded to Bradley Wiggins. He joins his young BMC comrade Tejay van Garderen and they push on hard, causing consternation behind.

Rogers puts his head down in inimitable style and cranks out a fearsome rhythm, taking Porte, Wiggins and Froome back up to the BMC pairing. The acceleration has served to kick the pain further down the mountain. Now it is the riders trying to hold on to the Team Sky quartet who are troubled.

The stage is set for a proper gunfight on La Toussuire. The remainder of the breakaway is now unlikely to be reeled in by the Tour grandees, but this is where the real race is, a minute or two behind the lone figure of Pierre Rolland as he battles towards yet another French stage win this week.

Richie Porte is the man charged by Sean Yates to set the tempo on the last climb of the day. The finish line is situated right at the top of the mountain, so Porte knows there will be no opportunity to pull back an attack on the descent: he must bury himself to ensure attacking is impossible.

Janez Brajkovič of Astana is the first to test Team Sky. He's joined in short order by Thibaut Pinot and the dangerous Belgian, Jurgen Van Den Broeck. Porte stays calm and pulls away on the front of the rapidly diminishing yellow jersey group, but when Vincenzo Nibali moves to join the attackers, it is clear that something must be done.

For the first time since the weekend, Team Sky's full armoury is called upon. Chris Froome, hunched over his handlebars like he's trying to pull his bike apart, shreds the group to nullify Nibali and Van Den Broeck. There are around 5km left to the top and the Tour de France could be won and lost in those precious minutes. Unfortunately for Australian fans, it looks like the man who will lose it today will be their hero, Cadel Evans. Froome's pace is just too much for the champion and he agonisingly loses contact with Wiggins and the race lead. For once not left totally exposed by his inadequate BMC team – supposedly the richest squad in cycling – he is forced to rely on his foot soldier van Garderen. Proudly clad in the white jersey that denotes the race's best-placed young rider, the American paces the distraught Evans to the finish. He will concede a minute and a half to those ahead, surely an insurmountable loss when added to his existing deficit.

As Froome nears Nibali's back wheel, the intense effort catches up with him and Wiggins pushes through to complete the recapture of the Italian himself. As the attack is finally snuffed out, the race eases imperceptibly, allowing Froome to regain the group.

Knowing that Evans is struggling behind, the group look to extend their advantage over him and the attacks keep coming. It is when countering one of these moves that Chris Froome kicks over the can of worms that will come to dominate the rest of this race. He shoots clear of his companions with a breathtaking kick that hurts everybody, his leader Wiggins included. He has covered no more than 100m more when he is seen talking into the mic attached to his jersey and sitting up, looking behind. He is clearly in touch with Sean Yates in the following car, and though the wording of the message he has received remains between them, the sentiment from Yates is clear: Don't you dare. Wait.

The loyal Froome does exactly that, rejoined by the yellow jersey seconds later. There's no question that it has been an uncomfortable moment for Wiggins. Was he attacked by his teammate? Was Froome just forcing the pace to increase the pressure on Nibali and Van Den Broeck? Was Froome just maximising the distance to Evans?

With only Rolland from the day's break ahead of them, the yellow jersey group at the finish consists of just Pinot, Froome, Van Den Broeck, Nibali and Wiggins.

Team Sky now hold first and second place overall, Froome having clambered over Evans in the standings. The Australian is now a distant fourth behind Vincenzo Nibali, 3'19" behind Bradley Wiggins.

The outcome could scarcely be better for Team Sky, but all the talk at La Toussuire is about Froome's 'attack' and a possible rivalry between the first- and second- placed teammates.

Amid the frantic speculation, cyclingnews.com's Peter Cossins summed up the situation calmly and accurately: 'There is no avoiding the conclusion that the rider most capable of toppling Wiggins is riding in the same team.'

BRADLEY WIGGINS HAD HIGH hopes for 2009. He managed to steady himself after the Beijing Olympics – he still enjoyed his fair share of parties, nights out and invitations to functions, but he was back in training a few months earlier than after his post-Athens blitz.

He was talking to the Garmin–Slipstream team about 2009. They were keen for him to express himself as a rider and properly fulfil his potential on the road, which they felt was something he was a long way off doing so far. The road was to be Brad's objective, for now at least, and further thoughts of Olympic glory on the track would be shelved until preparations for London 2012 needed discussing. The main topic of discussion was weight. The ideal weight for a track rider was generally slightly heavier than that of a roadman. While track performance was largely governed by power output, the key factor in road success was the ratio of power to weight. A ten-stone rider will need less power to get over a hill than a twelve-stone rider, goes the equation. Brad and his new Garmin-Slipstream team thought that he could lose the best part of a stone, as long as it was done carefully. Of course, he wasn't exactly overweight, so the careful part of that equation was crucial. It would need to be done with a careful mix of diet and training to avoid power and endurance ebbing away with that weight.

The season started with a very encouraging second to an unstoppable Alberto Contador in the Paris–Nice prologue, followed by good rides at Milan–San Remo, the Tour of Flanders and Paris–Roubaix. Cav won in San Remo, still his best ride outside the Tour de France and World Championships, and Brad took top 30 placings in both of the hard northern classics he was beginning to really enjoy riding. His third visit to the Giro d'Italia was something of a revelation, climbing being a much more comfortable experience for the slimmed-down 2009 version Wiggo. He was tempted to open the throttle out and cane it on many occasions, but continually reminded himself that the battlefield of the Tour de France would be the decisive point of his year, and held back accordingly. On the final day into Rome, with the family watching, he rode the perfect time trial and was surely destined for his greatest win as a professional until the weather intervened. Heavy rain meant a whole bunch of treacherous cobbled corners in the final kilometres and he forced himself to back off the gas with the bigger prizes looming on the horizon. A crash now simply wouldn't do. Brad was second to the Lithuanian Ignatas Konovalovas, who had finished before the rain came down.

That disappointment aside, the Briton was flying and champing at the bit to start his third Tour de France.

The prologue was in Monaco and featured a tough climb and tricky descent. Wiggins put his money on Cancellara and Contador and wasn't about to lose the bet. What was a bigger surprise to the field was the identity of the rider in third place on the evening of the first Saturday in July: Bradley Wiggins. Some believed that he was only a prologue specialist fulfilling his brief, but others sensed a new Wiggins. He looked thinner for starters, his gaunt face beginning to resemble a bird of prey, accentuating his roman nose into more of a beak in profile. The new Wiggins was perhaps more of a raptor.

Garmin-Slipstream were very strong in the time trial, an event which the organisers had strategically placed in Stage 4 of that year's Tour. With his high GC place from the prologue, a stage-winning ride in the time trial from Garmin-Slipstream could conceivably put Brad in the lead. The yellow jersey! It seemed inconceivable, and would surely be a temporary tenure until Alberto, Andy and Lance started slugging it out in the Pyrenees, but still . . .

It wasn't to be. On that infamous third stage to La Grand Motte, Bradley was one of the field that got caught on the wrong side of the split when HTC forced the pace into the crosswinds and the resulting lost seconds cost them the chance of a shot at yellow.

Garmin-Slipstream shrugged the disappointment aside and turned their attentions to that team time trial. With Brad, David Millar, Dave Zabriskie and Christian Vande Velde in their line-up, they had an incredible array of testers. The trick would be coaxing the other riders through, or, at least one of them: in the team time trial, the time is taken on the fifth man to cross the line. They were down to five early on after going out all guns blazing. The TV commentators thought they'd blown it, but the tactic was actually part of a plan, albeit a risky one. If that fifth rider, future Giro winner Ryder Hesjedal, or one of the four main men were to drop off, all their effort would be wasted. In the end, they were only bested by the Astana unit of Contador and Armstrong, who batted all the way down to nine in this discipline and brought the whole team home eighteen seconds ahead of Garmin-Slipstream. Four stages had gone, and Bradley was in sixth spot on the GC.

It was expected that Brad would begin a long descent down the rankings the next day, when the Tour took in its first big mountain top finish, the long, long drag up to Arcalis in Andorra used by Jan Ullrich to forge his sole Tour de France victory in 1997. But Bradley confounded the doubters by riding comfortably in the group of GC contenders all the way up the mountain, rubbing shoulders with Armstrong and the Schlecks. Those commentators had failed to take in the nature of that climb: it's long, all right, but without a proliferation of hairpins or steep ramps to break the rhythm. If ever a big mountain climb could be said to suit Bradley Wiggins, it would be Arcalis. Only at the top, when Alberto Contador sprang away unchallenged to put some time into his rivals did Brad lose sight of any of his opponents, but he wasn't alone. Contador was clearly head and shoulders above the rest of this race, regardless of any mind-games his teammate Armstrong might try. Brad was in the company of royalty, and people were beginning to notice.

A few days later, Alberto Contador was even paying him the compliment of telling the press that he would have to put time into Brad to avoid him being a danger to his yellow jersey in the late time trial in Annecy.

Bradley Wiggins found himself riding into the Alps as a genuine podium contender. The first day was a yomp up to Verbier in Switzerland, with Contador and Schleck going head to head and dropping the field before the classy Spaniard asserted himself upon the Luxembourger. Astonishingly, the new confident Bradley Wiggins took fifth place on the mountain, just over a minute behind the imperious race leader. He was in third overall, a place behind a man who had finished 25 seconds after him at Verbier, a chap by the name of Lance Armstrong.

Suddenly, the cycling press weren't asking when Wiggins would crack, but if he would at all. Contador, the consummate stage racer, wouldn't be expected to lose his 1'46" lead to Wiggins in the Annecy time trial, but it was not beyond the realms of possibility. Suddenly, the London track specialist was being spoken of as a potential Tour winner. It wasn't a cert, but it was definitely a possibility. They would have to shift him.

They had a damned good try at it on the next stage over the twin peaks of Grand and Petit Saint Bernard, when Andy Schleck shredded the field with a powerful attack. Only six men could stay with the pace, but one of those was Bradley Wiggins. He stayed third in Bourg-Saint-Maurice at 1'46".

The next day was another trial. There were only two opportunities for the climbers in the Tour de France to force their way into the reckoning: this stage to Le Grand-Bornan, and Saturday's sprawling epic to the summit of the Giant of Provence, Mont Ventoux. The Schlecks worked in tandem quite brilliantly, spread-eagling the entire field, with the notable exception of the simply brilliant Contador, who matched them the whole way. In the end, it suited all three of them to some extent: Frank Schleck won the stage, Contador retained the jersey, and all three of them saw Armstrong and Wiggins get bounced to give them sole occupancy of the podium places. Brad had slipped to sixth behind Contador, Andy, Frank, Lance and Andreas Klöden. It wasn't his best day, but he was proud of a stunning rearguard action that still left him in with a shout at a good finish. Coming into this race, his team had hopes of a top twenty finish for Brad, but also thought highly of Zabriskie, Vande Velde and Millar's chances. Now their weight was all behind Wiggins and he was still comfortably outstripping expectations in a dazzling sixth place overall.

Despite Mont Ventoux looming on the distant horizon, Brad was quietly confident of improving his position. He was loving every minute of being a player on the big stage and the fatigue was losing out to the excitement. He was strongly backing himself to bounce back in the time trial, feeling that he had ridden pretty well to Le Grand-Bornan and only been beaten by men he would always expect to lose time to in the circumstances. He was going to control the controllables and concentrate on the time trial, his domain.

Garmin had reconnoitred the time trial course on the rest day and discovered it to be a bit harder than the race manual suggested. The hill was longer and steeper, not ideal for Brad, but he would tackle it better prepared. A wind blew up during the course of the race, favouring the earlier starters. That meant a chance to shine for the time trial specialists who were low down on GC and thus starting well before the hitters. Fabian Cancellara fell into this category, as did David Millar, and they were among the top five. Only one of the overall contenders was able to pierce this block of testers: the man who would now certainly be crowned in Paris, the unsurpassable Alberto Contador. He was fastest of all, glorying in a stage win in the yellow jersey and proving beyond doubt that he was the strongest rider in this race. Nearest to him of his rivals was indeed the confident resurgent Wiggins, sixth at 42 seconds, inside the times of everybody in front of him on the overall standings save Contador. Klöden, Armstrong and both Schlecks all gave way to Garmin's Londoner who went to bed in fourth spot that night with only Mont Ventoux standing in his way.

The Tour de France organisers had played a blinder in keeping the podium places in question right up to the final weekend, and Bradley Wiggins was still a key player. What a Tour, what a rider.

Saint-Jean-de-Maurienne– Annonay Davézieux, 226km

Friday, 13 July 2012

The history of cycling is littered with lurid stories of teammates in rivalry.

The uniqueness of cycling lies in it being a team sport with individual winners. There are plenty of sports where a band of brothers join together in an all-for-one-one-for-all blood pact to overcome the obstacles placed in front of them, but those all end up with a team name engraved on the plinth around the base of a cup of some description; a City, a United, a Giants, a Lakers. Cycling is the only sport that demands that a team of professionals perform at the very peak of their ability with no hope of receiving eternal fame except to bask in the distant reflected glow of one of their number. It's his name that the engraver etches into the silverware, not the team's.

This is the fertile breeding ground that jealousy and self-belief thrive in. Why him? Why not me?

In 1985, Bernard Hinault won his record-equalling fifth Tour de France, thanks in no little part to the sterling work of his youthful American teammate, Greg LeMond. At his victory parade on the Champs-Élysées, incidentally the last by a French rider, Hinault promised to return the favour the following year. Horror and confusion could be seen on the guileless LeMond's face as his trusted mentor attacked him in the Pyrenees. With the La Vie Claire team split asunder, the English-speakers refusing to speak to the French-speakers and vice versa, open warfare raged between the two all the way to Alpe d'Huez where the older man fought in vain to distance the pretender. The rest of the field was blown away, left far back down the hairpins towards Le Bourg-d'Oisans, as the pair rode the mountain as if tied together by a short bootlace. All the way to the top, where *Le Blaireau* finally accepted it wasn't going to happen and crossed the line hand in hand with his comrade/enemy. Hinault was to claim that it was only correct that he challenge LeMond as the only other rider in the race capable of rendering the *arriviste*'s victory valid. Then he promptly retired.

The leader of the Carrera *squadra* for the 1987 Giro d'Italia was the pin-up of Italian cycling, Roberto Visentini. Some deft manoeuvring in the first week saw him take up ownership of the leader's pink jersey with the firm intention of carrying it all the way to Milan. That he wasn't able to do so was almost entirely down to the aggression of his Irish lieutenant Stephen Roche who rode himself into the lead, firmly believing that his was the better claim to greatness and Visentini would only lose the race for Carrera if left to carry on unmolested. The *tifosi* were outraged, lining the Dolomites to aim punches at the usurper, protected only by his one loyal teammate, the Belgian Eddy Schepers and a man who was supposedly his rival, the Scottish climber on the Panasonic team, Robert Millar. Millar was to some extent driven by hubris having previously been robbed of overall victory at the Vuelta on the penultimate day by a cabal of Spaniards unwilling to see an Anglo take their race away. The promise of rides for both men on the superteam Roche was building for the following season also helped. As if to make his point, Roche went on to win the Tour and the World Championships that year as well, only the second man since the great Merckx himself to pull off that feat. It broke him though, and his *annus mirabilis* never came remotely close to being repeated.

As recently as 2009 Bradley Wiggins had watched from inside the yellow jersey group as Alberto Contador and Lance Armstrong kicked lumps out of each other for a couple of weeks before Armstrong accepted the inevitable and gave ground to the younger man. It was scarcely believable that they both wore the name of Astana across their jerseys such was their obvious rivalry and antipathy.

So what of Wiggins and Froome? The party line was clear: Froome's time will come, the 2012 Tour de France is all about Bradley Wiggins as far as Team Sky are concerned.

The riders all smiled and hugged back at the team bus last night, delighted that the outcome of the day couldn't have been better for Team Sky. The top two riders in the Tour were Team Sky men. Nibali had been neutralised, Evans distanced. This race was past its halfway point with many big mountains encountered and handled. The Tour de France was Team Sky's to lose.

However, somebody had forgotten to inform the twittering classes.

'Oh SNAP!' tweeted David Millar through virtually audible fits of giggles. 'Sky have WAG WAR on twitter. This shit just got real.'

You'd think that somebody would have had a word with the Team Sky wives-and-girlfriends after Mark Cavendish's girlfriend Peta Todd stirred up the gossipers earlier in the race when she accused his team of not supporting her man. But she isn't the only Team Sky WAG with a Twitter account.

Immediately after yesterday's stage and his apparent reining in by the team, Chris Froome's girlfriend, the South African sports photographer Michelle Cound, tweeted 'Beyond disappointed. I know what happened just then.'

Still fuming later on and presumably pondering her man's chance of winning the Tour de France being refused him, she added: 'If you want loyalty, get a Froome dog . . . a quality I value . . . although being taken advantage of by others!'

Anybody who has had the good fortune to encounter Cath Wiggins will know that the leader's wife is a big character not afraid to show her feelings. She's articulate and insightful. That means there can be little chance that her pointed omission of Froome's name when she listed her husband's helpers at La Toussuire was accidental, especially when it hit the tweetdeck shortly after Cound's outspoken remarks. Mrs Wiggins wrote: 'See Mick Rogers and Richie Porte for examples of genuine, selfless effort and true professionalism.'

That would have been a PR disaster enough for Team Sky, but it was about to get worse. In no doubt that this was a slight on her earlier complaint, Michelle Cound chose to retweet Cath Wiggins's 'loyalty' pronouncement, preceding it with just one word: 'Typical!'

David Millar, having a good laugh over at the Garmin-Sharp hotel, wasn't the only one. As the likeable Simon MacMichael wrote on road.cc, 'On Twitter everybody can hear you scream.'

Wiggins himself was inevitably drawn into the exchanges, although he was more careful than the respective spouses to stay on message: 'Great day today for Team Sky, boys rode incredible today and Chris Froome super strong, big day behind us.'

The best tweet on the whole matter came yet again from the writer and different kind of wag, Richard Moore: 'Just trying to imagine the Kathy LeMond/Martine Hinault exchange had twitter been around during @1986Tour.'

★

The mountains have exacted a heavy toll on the race and no team suffered more than Rabobank. The Dutch superteam have lost three riders overnight when we roll out of the valley town of Saint-Jean-de-Maurienne this morning. Serial minor-placing sprinter Mark Renshaw hasn't made it and neither has his Dutch teammate Bauke Mollema. But by far the biggest blow is the loss of their star, the leader Robert Gesink. The skinny climber's chances have been talked up year on year for a while as he developed out of a mercurial prodigious *grimpeur* into someone who can supposedly challenge the best in a three-week tour. His fans are left waiting another year to see the hoped-for metamorphosis that we've all heard so much about.

Meanwhile, Dutch bookies are laughing all the way to the bank.

Another little problem no longer troubling Bradley Wiggins this morning is his minor spat with Vincenzo Nibali. It appears to be over after the leader showed the grace of the *patrons* of old by reaching out in a gesture of camaraderie and congratulations to his Italian rival as they crossed the finish line on La Toussuire yesterday afternoon. He may have felt that he had a little ground to make up after inadvertently 'disrespecting' Nibali the day before. If so, the pat on the shoulder seems to have done the trick. It seems Wiggins had sought out Nibali earlier in the day to explain that he meant no ill. 'That's the beauty of cycling right there,' said a happier Nibali. 'We can talk calmly and clear things up amongst ourselves. Wiggins has been a great rival. And he has a great teammate in Froome.'

Brad and Team Sky, especially the pacemakers of Christian Knees, Edvald Boasson Hagen, Mick Rogers and Richie Porte, have their fingers crossed that Stage 12 will be the 'day off' they've been hoping for. The stage profile – two big Alpine passes followed by a long float down into the Ardèche – is made for the long breakaway. 'It's going to be a hard first hour while everybody tries to get away, but then we might get things a bit easier now the race has settled down,' predicts Sean Yates.

He's almost note-perfect. The daily morning attacks fly, frantic enough for experienced Frenchman David Moncoutié to crash on the descent of the first mountain, the Col du Grand Cucheron, while trying to bridge to the front of the race. He writes himself out of any further participation in this race.

The only part not foreseen by the Team Sky DS was that Peter Sagan would get himself into one of the moves. He has his eyes on the green jersey points on offer at the day's intermediate sprint. It all gets a little bit quick for half an hour on the front as Team Sky are joined by Orica-GreenEDGE who are keen to bring the Slovak back. Their man Matt Goss is a challenger for that green jersey and they don't want to give Sagan an easy ride. Once the move is reeled in and the sprinters fight over those scraps, the race rolls on at a more sedate pace, up to twelve minutes behind a group of stage-hunters.

These are the days that Tour riders love. The mountains behind them for the moment, the transitional stages are a chance to roll their legs over and regain some strength after a horrible few days. They even get a chance to talk to each other.

Of the men up the road, the best known is Brad's old oppo and teammate, David Millar. This kind of day is the type that the Brit would have had a long hard look at when the Tour route was announced before Christmas. He would have calculated that the peloton would not be so interested in racing hard, and that he himself would be trailing the leader by some significant time after passing though the Alps. He was correct: he's in 93rd spot now, nearly an hour and a half behind Wiggins and no danger to the top ten. He's won on days like this before, knowledge safely in the locker if it should come down to a sprint from a small group.

The trick in these situations is to keep the group together as long as possible so that they have the best chance of staying away. This is best done by getting the composition of the breakaway correct – everybody should feel that they can win, nobody should have a teammate with them, there should be no big names well placed on GC. Millar has managed to surround himself with Jean-Christophe Péraud, Egoi Martínez, Cyril Gautier and Robert Kišerlovski. Textbook.

The quintet manage to get to within 4km of the line before they begin to look nervously at each other. The fact that they are still seven minutes ahead of the main event doesn't help, as they are under no pressure to hurry. Kišerlovski's nerve breaks first and he goes for the long one, possibly just hoping to shed one or two others to make the odds better for the sprint. He is recaptured and Martínez gives it a go. It's Péraud's move that cracks them, however. He goes clear, as the remaining four will each other to lead the chase.

David Millar expertly delays his pursuit for a moment to give the Frenchman an opportunity to establish a gap, then deftly covers it while the others squabble over the responsibility of chasing.

The newly formed duo share the effort of making good their escape, no mean feat after five and a half hours of bike riding. They stay equal until there are barely 500m left to the finish line, where Jean-Christophe Péraud plays his card. He refuses to pass, forcing the Garmin-Sharp rider to lead out the sprint, intending no doubt to pop over him in the last few yards like Chris Hoy.

You'll be lucky, son. David Millar has won three stages of this race over the years, and riders from Britain have already won three of this year's edition. His nous has only grown over the years since his last win here, back in 2003, and his speed has hardly diminished. Millar stays glued to the crowd barriers on his left and looks over his right shoulder, leaving no room for a surprise attack from his rival. Péraud makes his move with just 200m remaining, an all-out 100% commitment to reach the line first. The man coming off the wheel of the leader always has an advantage, though this decreases at lower speeds, as they both have to jump. For fans watching in Britain on TV there is a heart-in-mouth moment as Péraud goes round their man, but it is only a second before Millar's long legs get on top of the gear, and from that point there can be only one winner.

The fourth British winner at this Tour de France, and this on the anniversary of the original British yellow jersey hope's death on the brutal flanks of Mont Ventoux 45 years ago. Tom Simpson's ghost must be looking down on this race with a proud smile.

MONT VENTOUX HAS A special place in the history of cycling, and British cycling in particular. It's not the highest of mountains, but it sits in its own glorious isolation high above Avignon and the surrounding Provençale countryside, unencumbered by the range of brothers, sisters and cousins that make views of, say, Mont Blanc awkward to obtain. On a clear day Mont Ventoux is visible from every direction from many miles.

The weather is more likely to be clear here than in the less predictable Alps or Pyrenees, but that doesn't necessarily make it a pleasant place to be. When riders ascend from the village of Bédoin, they are protected by a canopy of trees up to the heights of Chalet Reynard, then it is an exposed crawl across the barren white shoulder of rock all the way to the blasted outcrop on which sits the red-and-white-striped tower of the observatory that marks the summit. Exposure is the name of the game, and the mountain can be blazingly hot or perishingly cold, even in July. Not for nothing does its name loosely translate as the windy mountain. When Armstrong and Pantani rode to this summit in the 2000 Tour de France, the press were forced to decamp to the foot of the climb as it was too windy to erect the mobile *salle du presse*. It must have been the shortest podium ceremony in cycling history, Armstrong stiffly waving his golden stuffed lion in a pair of thermal tights then racing out of the freezing gale to the comfort of his motor home.

It was of course here in 1967 that the dreams of victory of Britain's great Tour de France hope, Tom Simpson, faltered along with the great man's heart. He died on these dry slopes, wedded for eternity to the cause. His famous last words echo down across the decades. 'Put me back on my bike,' he demanded after his first collapse on those fatal slopes. Minutes later, he was gone forever, but he will never, ever be forgotten.

Tom Simpson died for many reasons: exhaustion, the heat, amphetamines, brandy . . . Any number of factors can be brought up as the cause of his demise, but anybody who has suffered on a bicycle will appreciate that the true reason Tom Simpson died was that his will was stronger than his body. Most of us know when it's time to give up. Our body tells us that we can't do it any more. Stop, get off, wait, walk, or just slow down a bit, it may sound 'soft' but ultimately it's just common sense. The ability to ignore those sensible warnings is what sets great champions apart from good athletes. Tom Simpson was the best there has ever been at bearing that pain, and he paid for it with his life.

The memorial to Tom on the high slopes of Ventoux is a shrine for cyclists of all types, but especially the huge numbers of people who venture south from Britain to test themselves against the mountain that claimed his life and to pay their own respects, even forty or more years after he was taken from us.

On the last day of true combat in the 2009 Tour de France, Bradley Wiggins was looking to pay his own special tribute to the memory of Tom Simpson by riding to the top of that very mountain without losing the company of the elite riders he had shadowed for three weeks. Bucking the formbook, expectation and his own lack of history in the world's greatest race, he was determined to ride into Paris the following day as the first Englishman to finish fourth in the Tour de France.

There were a few people who wanted to stop him. Lance Armstrong's comeback bid to win an unprecedented eighth Tour de France may have ended in failure, but the Texan still had a podium finish to hang on to, and making that safe didn't involve helping Bradley Wiggins. Andreas Klöden was only two seconds behind Brad on GC and would love to grab back the time that Wiggins had stolen off him in the Annecy time trial. Even more dangerous was the resurgent Frank Schleck, keen to get as close to his brother as possible, and possibly shoulder Armstrong, Wiggins and Klöden all aside to join his younger brother below Contador on the podium in Paris. He had been climbing brilliantly in this final week and already had a great stage victory to his name. He needed just 23 small seconds to clamber over Brad and Klöden. Even Vincenzo Nibali, at less than two minutes, could not be disregarded on the slopes of the bald mountain.

Unsurprisingly, Frank is the first to move. He jumps out of the rapidly diminishing yellow jersey group but is comfortably countered by Armstrong, and the others regain the duo's back wheels. Next Andy goes, not really attacking Contador – he is four minutes behind – but looking to unhitch Klöden, Wiggins and Armstrong in favour of his brother. Contador takes up long-term residence on his wheel and won't shift until prised off it by *soigneurs* at the finish. Frank tries again, and this one is fierce. Klöden is hating this and regains the group by the skin of his teeth. Only Andy, Frank, Contador, Armstrong, Wiggins, Nibali and Klöden remain, and the German is in agony.

Andy attacks once more, Contador on him like flypaper. Frank and Armstrong stare each other down and let the move go, Brad following in their wheel tracks. Nibali bridges across to the front two. If they decide to go for the stage and catch Juan Manuel Gárate, the long-time leader, this could be a problem. Andy sits up though, conscious that his brother isn't there. The group reforms.

The brothers try to go together this time. Armstrong covers, much to Frank's visible frustration. What does he have to do? This is one acceleration too much for the brave Klöden and he finally loses his grasp on the group. Wiggins makes it, but it's a massive effort and he is in obvious discomfort. The wheels in front start to drift away from him and his head bobs alarmingly as he tries everything to stay with them.

Bravo, Brad! screams the ghost of Tom Simpson in his ear, as he somehow finds the power to grind back up to the Schlecks, Contador and Armstrong. Klöden has blown; Nibali is struggling but still there. The final battle for this brilliant Tour will take place over this last kilometre.

Andy surges forward one more time, and only Contador and Armstrong can follow. Frank puts his head down and slowly but surely opens a gap on Brad. Frank has overtaken Klöden on GC for sure, and only needs 24 seconds to overhaul Bradley Wiggins for fourth spot.

Come on, Brad! *Come on!*

The cameras focus on the finish line, where Gárate hangs on for the greatest win of his career. The Schlecks, Alberto Contador and Lance Armstrong cross together, the final peace treaty drawn up amid a mutual admiration for each other's performance.

But where's Brad? The clock is ticking. Please, Mr TV Director, show us Brad. Here he comes! Come on! Come on, Brad! It's going to be close. Where the hell is that finish line?

Bradley Wiggins hauls himself over the line on top of Mont Ventoux in four hours, 40 minutes and 24 seconds. That is twenty seconds behind Frank Schleck. He will hold on to his fourth place in Paris. After nearly 3,500km of racing, three slender seconds separate him from Frank Schleck in fifth.

Chapeau, Mr Wiggins! says the ghost of Tom Simpson.

Saint-Paul-Trois-Châteaux–Le Cap d'Agde, 217km

Saturday, 14 July 2012

There is only one team in this Tour de France that is yet to place a rider in a breakaway of any kind. This is most likely because they are desperately trying to control such occurrences and need all hands to the pump, especially after being reduced to eight men early in the race.

It is of course Team Sky we're talking about. Both their main objectives – keeping the race together to protect the lead of Bradley Wiggins and getting Mark Cavendish to the end of flat stages in a position to win the sprint – require control of breaks.

However, the Spanish Movistar team director José Luis Arrieta has a different theory about the British squad's absence in moves. It's because Team Sky, like every other team in the Tour, can only have two cars in the race and one of them, according to Arrieta, has to be with Mark Cavendish at all times. 'The sprinter and World Champion always requires a team car for when he gets dropped,' Arrieta told the Spanish daily *El País*. This view of Cavendish as something of a prima donna is at odds with the daily shots of the rainbow jersey trekking back through the bunch to gather drinks for all his teammates then distributing them with the care and diligence of a devoted butler. But Arrieta is confident in his view that Team Sky don't just put Bernie Eisel at Cav's disposal, but a Jaguar and crew, too. He thinks that this personal backroom is at the root of the lack of Team Sky attacks, as there is no other car to slot in behind such a move to offer assistance. 'Since each team has a maximum of two vehicles, and one must be with the team leader, that prevents Froome launching an attack or another like Boasson Hagen or Knees.'

Team Sky would like to win today's stage, but they're not planning on doing it via the medium of the long breakaway. They have a Plan A and also a Plan B, but first the day's primary objective must be achieved: the security of the yellow jersey.

Sean Yates and Dave Brailsford prepare the team for the day's tribulations behind the blacked-out windows of the Team Sky bus with as much care as any day. 'The big issue today is going to be crosswinds. There's a run in to the Cap along the coast that's a big open area. Forecast will be for cross-head-winds, so be aware. Don't get caught in the wrong part of the bunch if it splits,' warns Yates.

The crosswinds are perennial issues on days like today. An alert HTC squad led by Mick Rogers famously put the cat among the pigeons during Lance Armstrong's comeback Tour de France in 2009. The old stager was cagey enough to sense what was about to happen as the peloton was struck by some heavy winds and the entire HTC squad moved to the front and put the pedal to the metal. His 'co-leader' and defending champion Alberto Contador was less astute, as Rogers and his HTC hitmen pulled the race apart and caused not only a split in the field but a split in the Astana team camp. By the finish – naturally won by Mark Cavendish to make it mission accomplished for HTC – Armstrong was claiming that his newly won lead over Contador ought to make him the more privileged and protected Astana rider.

The danger with the wind is that when one rider loses contact with the wheel in front, it quickly becomes extremely difficult to bridge that gap. If that happens to several riders at once, as is often the case, there can suddenly be four or five groups on the road. A rider can lose time without getting dropped, just being caught in the wrong group. Awareness is everything, hence Brailsford and Yates's attempts to drum the message home and their close examination of the day's *parcours*.

When the race meets the coastal strip, just a little way along the seafront from that day in 2009, Team Sky are all diligently in their places near the front. It's been a relatively easy day for the troops so far, as Orica-GreenEDGE have once again taken up much of the chasing to hunt down the day's break. They've got nothing out of this race so far, and with Simon Gerrans their highest-placed rider in the GC, a lowly 62nd, a stage win is imperative. Matt Goss has come close a couple of times. He's a great sprinter from a group, but it remains unproven as to whether he can really beat the fastest guys on a level playing field. However, today's route features a short but sharp little climb along that stretch of coast and the Orica-GreenEDGE boss Neil Stephens is working on the assumption that many of the fastest finishers will be shelled out of the rear of the race by the high speeds and gradient.

Another Australian with action on his mind is the proud champion Cadel Evans. Normally, a transitional second-week stage in the Tour between the Alps and Pyrenees would see the favourites biding their time, conserving their energy and waiting for something to happen. In his earlier days, Evans was considered a conservative rider, but we had to rip up that view of him after his daring attack to win the 2009 World Championships at Mendrisio in Switzerland. The devastating move to crush an elite lead group of hitters surprised everyone and the rainbow jersey brought a transformation in the previously 'boring, boring Evans'. It was this new attacking Cadel Evans who won the 2011 Tour de France rather than the Mk 1 serial second-and-third-placed Evans.

So, it shouldn't surprise us when he makes his move approaching the small climb of Mont Saint Clair, punctuating the coastal route between Montpellier and Le Cap d'Agde, but there is a stirring of excitement nevertheless. Neil Stephens's prediction is correct, and several fast men slip away from the front group. Bradley Wiggins and his men cruise up behind the adventurous Evans without any great hardship, but Team Sky's Plan A for today is in tatters, as the rainbow jersey of Mark Cavendish is one of the many distanced by the reduced peloton as it flies up the hill at the sort of pace that most of us reserve for coming down the other side of such obstacles.

This is great news for Orica-GreenEDGE, who continue to not only seek to position Matt Goss for the finish, but also throw the lively Michael Albasini on the attack. A sight that won't have pleased Stephens's men quite so much is the line of Lotto Belisol riders taking over the pacemaking at the head of the race. That can only mean one thing: Andre Greipel has not suffered the fate of Cavendish, and he is still in the front group. That's not all … The green jersey of Liquigas-Cannondale's Peter Sagan is also spotted hanging in at the business end of affairs. Goss could well have done with seeing the back of them. To be brutal, all he's done is see the back of them as they cross finish lines just ahead of him for the last week or two.

For Team Sky, it's time for Plan B. The crosswinds are at their stiffest along this last stretch of rather grim industrial coastal strip towards Agde. It's like the Camargue but in some Ballardian post-apocalyptic future, with power lines and the occasional warehouse standing in for white bulls and flamingos. We can see a Team Sky rider in a white jersey holding his place in their line as they cruise along with the faster teams at the front, but it's not the pattern of the rainbow around it, it's the flag of Norway, and Edvald Boasson Hagen is wearing it.

As the bunch snakes its way at silly speeds into the narrow streets and corners of the last couple of kilometres, Team Sky hit the front to stretch the race to its limits for the Norwegian. But it's not a black, blue and white Team Sky jersey on the front, or even the Norwegian Champion's top. Incredibly, it's the race leader himself, Bradley Marc Wiggins in the yellow jersey and yellow helmet, his stealthy black Pinarello wearing yellow detail in honour of his status, leaving the whole Tour de France gasping for breath as they attempt to follow his acceleration in aid of his teammate.

Boasson Hagen blasts off his leader's wheel in search of the line with a mighty effort, but it's not quite enough to beat those pesky sprinters. Greipel and Sagan finish one and two, with Boasson Hagen taking a fine third place behind them to add to his brace of second spots in the opening week. For all Orica-GreenEDGE's superb efforts to take the race by the scruff of the neck, they have to settle for Daryl Impey's fifth in the sprint.

Greipel is particularly pleased by his win due to his scaling of Mont Saint Clair with the main field when many of his rivals, Cavendish being the most notable, were unable to follow. It may not have proved that he is the fastest sprinter, but he would argue that he is the better cyclist. It is an argument that won't be settled today, but this win is a tick in his column without a doubt.

At Team Sky, there is muted satisfaction with the day. Morale is on a high after everybody's efforts for the popular Edvald Boasson Hagen and the leader's show of strength to set up a valued teammate has set the media purring. Bradley himself is coy about his ride that recalls his DS Yates in his juss-doin'-me-job heyday.

'It was just the last kilometre, slightly downhill,' he said dismissively of his big lead out for Boasson Hagen. 'It was the safest place to be and I just wanted to repay a friend of mine.'

Sean Yates reflected on the quiet contentment in the camp. Speaking to the Team Sky website, he said, 'It was a technical finish with a few roundabouts. Brad had to be at the front in case it split, which we actually saw heading into the 3km mark. Froomey was right there too so all in all it was a good performance. It was nice to see Bradley leading out Edvald at the finish,' he added with a touch of personal pride for a job well done.

Brad reiterated the team's professionalism and commitment to the job in hand. 'You have to pay attention to every single day, even a day like today because of the bends in the last 400m. You have to be careful every day until Paris.'

○

GARMIN–SLIPSTREAM AND BRADLEY WIGGINS followed up his superb 2009 Tour de France ride in belligerent fashion, silencing the whispers about his perceived leap in performance by openly publishing his blood tests for the whole of 2009. They clearly displayed the level, even results one would expect to see in an athlete untainted by chemical stimulus.

They were trying to reinforce the point that Brad's improvement was based upon simple hard work, weight loss and improved confidence. For the first time in his career he was a total road racer and had seen a complete turnaround in his performance as a result.

'I don't want there to be any suspicion or doubt that what I did was natural. I have nothing to hide and I want this transparency,' explained Brad in the post–Tour scrum of attention, asking that the team publish the 'blood passport' that all riders need to demonstrate their lack of doping.

Garmin-Slipstream had been tremendously supportive and had played a major part in Bradley's transformation from track star to Tour contender. He was contracted to them for another season, but he wouldn't have been human if he hadn't been fully aware of developments in Great Britain.

Dave Brailsford, such a driving force behind Brad's career and the stellar success of the Team GB World Championship and Olympic programme, had launched the monolithic Team Sky upon the world. The team would begin racing in 2010 and nobody doubted Brailsford's promises that it would be the most professional, efficient racing unit the world had ever seen. It would be a British-based team supporting British riders, providing a conduit for those cyclists who had progressed through the national ranks and were now seeking success on the road. The British riders would be joined by the cream of the world's available cycling talent.

It was that availability question that was getting everybody talking. Britain's two best cyclists, the raw emerging talent of Mark Cavendish and the polished, stylish Bradley Wiggins, were contracted to Team Columbia and Garmin-Slipstream respectively. When Team Sky began announcing that riders of the class of Edvald Boasson Hagen would be accompanying British talent like Geraint Thomas and Steve Cummings, Wiggins and Cavendish were the elephants in the room. How could it be a Best of British without them? And who would this 'British rider winning the Tour de France within five years' be if it wasn't going to be Bradley Wiggins?

More than that, Brailsford had been personally instrumental in both men's careers, nurturing them carefully through the ranks. He was especially close to Wiggins, who would have been uncertain of winning any of his multiple world and Olympic titles without the direct assistance of Brailsford and UK Cycling.

The will-he-won't-he saga dragged on for much of the remainder of 2009. At one time, Brad would describe reports of him moving to Team Sky as 'bollocks'; at another, he would cryptically refer to the difference in budget between the two outfits by saying, 'It's like trying to win the Champions League. You need to be at Manchester United, but I'm playing at Wigan at the moment. I've had a good time at Garmin, but times have changed.'

The old Wiggins hobby of provocatively toying with the press when answering repetitive questions reared its head when asked about a Team Sky contract for the umpteenth time: 'I've still got a contract with Sky for about another year. The wife wants the movie package, and I've just got the sports package at the moment. We'll see. The kids like all the cartoons like Disney Channel and all that, so we'll probably keep it for another year. But I think TNT has a new package when you can get the movies, the sports channels and all the other stuff for like a combo value; it's 49 quid a month. We'll see. I don't know. I'm thinking of changing my Garmin to Tom-Tom as well.'

It was therefore no big surprise when, after weeks of behind-the-scenes wrangling and coy public statements, Team Sky announced the transfer of Bradley Wiggins from Garmin-Slipstream for the 2010 season. They had forked out £2m to free him from his contract for the coming season and had reportedly tripled Wiggins's salary to one that they felt befitted a genuine Tour de France contender. They now had their leader.

There had been a noticeable cooling of the relationship between Wiggins and the press over the latter half of 2009. The cycling journalists who were now following his every move were a different breed to the BBC and national press who came out of the woodwork around Olympic time and generally paid cyclists no heed otherwise. The problem with the latter, as far as Wiggins and his ilk were concerned, was a lack of under-standing of their sport and the tendency to patronise or unin-tentionally belittle the subjects of their interviews. The issue with cycling journalists was a much more intrusive one. These guys were proper hardened hacks with column inches to fill every day and every week. They wanted stories, gossip, dirt and scandal. And unlike their more generally minded counter-parts, there was nothing these people didn't know about the sport.

The post-2009 Tour Wiggins was a wary beast, a reticent creature, especially in light of his rent-a-quote past. Journalists who had known him a long time scratched their heads at the transformation, but it wasn't completely mystifying. Brad was protecting himself and his family as he saw it, playing his cards closer to his chest in an effort to avoid his words being twisted or taken out of context. The downside was that he appeared to be unhappy and unfriendly as a result, just when he was expected to be delighted and excited about his new team. The Team Sky launch turned out to be a rather uncomfortable affair with Brad fending questions without the banter that had accompanied previous similar events. Brailsford alongside him seemed uncertain of how to play it and ended up similarly downbeat. It was all a bit strange.

Stories circulated about Brad being petulant at official team duties such as photo shoots. With the rest of the team behaving immaculately, his attitude stood out all the more. He was clearly not enjoying his part in the media circus of the new team. Maybe he just wanted to be racing again. During this down time in his year either side of Christmas, he would often have been involved with the track squad with the aim of medals at next season's big tournaments but, for now, track riding was in his past.

He'd joined Team Sky to win the Tour de France.

STAGE 14:

Limoux–Foix, 191km

Sunday, 15 July 2012

Vandalism, civil disobedience and protest have a long history in sport, and the Tour de France has had more than its fair share over the decades.

Just like the 'George Davis is Innocent' campaigners who dug up the Headingley pitch overnight before the final day of the 1975 Ashes Test with the Australians on the ropes, there are sometimes unusual outcomes. On that day, the Aussies were grateful to the alleged armed robber's supporters as the match was abandoned and they scraped a draw at the last Test to take the Ashes 1–0.

Bernard Hinault – he seems to crop up so often in stories – was at the sharp end of the dispute with striking shipyard workers on the Col d'Eze during the 1984 Paris–Nice race. As the men jumped about in the road, bringing the race to a stand-still, a bewildered rider was grabbed by one of the protestors. The Badger rushed up and gave the interloper a knuckle sandwich full in the chops.

At Courchevel in the 2000 Tour de France, an ingenious bunch of nutters jumped the barriers complete with bikes and clad in the outfits of their heroes. As Marco Pantani soloed towards the top of the mountain, he was suddenly and unaccountably caught by Fernando Escartín. The Spanish climber had appeared out of nowhere – almost literally it was revealed, as it wasn't Escartín, but a punter clad in Kelme replica kit. The always excitable finish line voices of Phil Liggett and Paul Sherwen were entirely flummoxed. The commentators were also completely thrown when a pretty convincing fake Lance Armstrong joined a small group sprinting for the minor placings. A similarly counterfeit Richard Virenque was clearly not on the same juice as the real King of the Mountains as he was easily outpaced by the confused pros.

In 2009, a mass participation event in Perthshire attracting 3,500 riders was targeted by a local church elder unhappy about not being able to drive to Sunday service that morning. He scattered up to 10,000 carpet tacks upon that road, causing hundreds of punctures, untold withdrawals and the suspension of the event.

This last instance of protestation is particularly apt today. Somebody at the roadside on the top of the first category Mur de Péguère decides to pull a similar stunt. The difference lay in the numbers involved – it looks like a box of tacks rather than a shopful – and the fact that this isn't a public Sunday out, this is the world's biggest annual sporting event.

A day meandering through the beautiful *départements* of Aude and Ariège has taken the Tour de France into the Pyrenees. There are two big passes to climb, both on typically small winding Pyrenean lanes, but this isn't the classic monster mountain stage. You'll just have to wait a couple of days for that. A select group of classy riders who are nonetheless not dangerous to the overall standings has been allowed by Team Sky and the other teams shepherding the peloton to escape.

The sense of comradeship at Team Sky that has been carefully nurtured for the past two weeks in spite of the tweeting about internal rivalries is further enhanced after yesterday's big team effort for Edvald Boasson Hagen. Today Mark Cavendish is getting in on the act, as the World Champion rides up alongside his leader Bradley Wiggins and calmly tows the yellow jersey and the rest of the race up the first big Pyrenean climb of the day, the pretty Port de Lers. It is an impressive self-effacing piece of work by the avowed non-climber, who will end up crossing the line in 148th place today, nearly half an hour behind the leaders in *l'autobus*.

With nearly 40km left to cover from the top of the second big climb, the Mur de Péguère to the finish in the valley town of Foix, this isn't a particularly dangerous route for the leaders, but they are still looking at each other cautiously as they crest the narrow summit of the pass. It is now that Cadel Evans punctures. His team car trapped behind the long peloton as it squeezed over the top of the hill, Evans waits a horribly uncomfortable minute and fifteen seconds before he is able to pursue the men who have left him behind. But then he punctures again. And then, almost comically, a third time. The Australian must feel like the man in the dream who walks into a classroom and realises he has forgotten to put his trousers on, such is the nightmarishness of his situation.

It is clear that something odd is going on. Evans's teammate, the experienced New Yorker George Hincapie, will later confess to having 'never seen anything like it'. Up to 30 punctures strike the group. The most serious incident claims the participation in this Tour of the excellent Robert Kišerlovski of Astana, the Croatian climber hitting the tarmac after getting a flat and crashing out of the race with a broken collarbone.

On the narrow descent, the lucky ones that have avoided the beastly tacks quickly realise that all is not well. Race radio has gone berserk, the team directors stuck on the wrong side of the mountain behind the race are all bellowing into their own radios to find out if their riders are affected, and the bunch are all seen putting one finger into their ears or grabbing buttons attached to their jerseys as they try to get some understanding of what is happening behind them.

Without knowing it, Bradley Wiggins is about to cement his reputation as a worthy leader and true sportsman. He immediately slows the descent and quickly and calmly spreads the word to those around him that there is trouble behind affecting Evans among others, effectively neutralising the race.

'I just thought it was the honourable thing to do to wait for Cadel. No one wants to benefit from someone else's misfortune,' he shrugs later.

This unwritten rule has had its fair share of action over the years in the Tour: Lance Armstrong waiting for Jan Ullrich after a crash coming down the Col de Peyresourde in the central Pyrenees, Ullrich waiting for Armstrong after another mishap, the bunch waiting for Marco Pantani to get back up to them after a puncture on Alpe d'Huez. But there have been times when it has controversially not been adhered to, most infamously two years ago on the misty wet top of the Pyrenean giant, the Col du Tourmalet, when Alberto Contador took one look at Andy Schleck's dropped chain and shot off to gain a 39-second advantage on the stage. Just to rub salt into the aggrieved Luxembourger's wounds, Contador's advantage over the second-placed Schleck in Paris was exactly 39 seconds.

One man who is clearly not so keen on the chivalric code is Thomas Voeckler's Europcar teammate, Pierre Rolland. The Frenchman launches an attack on the descent after Wiggins had brought the race under control with the consent of his rivals, then tries again after they bring him back. His claims that he knew nothing of Evans's difficulties or of any other riders in trouble mark Rolland as either being economical with *la vérité* or perhaps being the most vacant rider in the bunch.

A grateful Evans regains the bunch as they coast towards the beautiful little Roman outpost of Foix. They are now an improbable eighteen minutes behind the lead group, where the breakaway riders are trying to figure out how they can eject the green jersey of intrepid Peter Sagan from their midst. The key is held by the crafty Luis Leon Sanchez, who times his attack to perfection to solo into the finish and take his third Tour de France victory. After spending as much time on the deck as in the saddle during the first week, the second week has been an active one for the Spanish break specialist as he tried continuously to land a stage.

Indeed, it is a day of redemption for his Rabobank team. The Dutch outfit is the longest continuous sponsor in the sport and is renowned for the amount of cash they pour in at all levels in the Netherlands, but due to a host of misfortunes they have been left with just four riders in this race. Today all four of the survivors finish near the front of the race, giving them an improbable shot in the arm by not only taking the stage but the mantle of best team on the day.

Cadel Evans gives a signal of thanks to Bradley Wiggins, Team Sky and the other riders who waited for him on the descent of the Mur de Péguère as the big group crosses the line. The tack talk is about to begin in earnest.

Unsurprisingly, Evans's sporting director at BMC Jean Lelangue is among the first to wade in for some forthright condemnation of the mystery perpetrator, stating that 'it was a criminal act by hooligans'. It's difficult to disagree with that conclusion, or the one offered by the man who had only enhanced his reputation on an afternoon of high drama and tension, Bradley Wiggins. 'What can you do? It's something we can't control. It's sad, but those are the type of things we have to put up with as cyclists. If that happened in a football stadium or wherever, you'd be arrested and seen on CCTV. But we are out there quite vulnerable at times; very close to the public on climbs.'

Not keen on puffing his chest out on the subject of his sportsmanship, Brad was nevertheless persuaded to find some words on Pierre Rolland's behaviour. 'I thought it was a little bit uncouth at that time. So many guys punctured at once, it became quite apparent very quickly that something was up. He didn't just attack once, he attacked twice. It didn't seem very honourable.'

The Tour de France has suffered at times in the absence of the traditional *patron* of years gone by, a leader who is universally respected and can be expected to make decisions on behalf of the whole bunch where necessary. In the old days this would have been Merckx or Hinault. Armstrong had authority but not a general mandate, and his contemporaries Johan Museeuw and Mario Cipollini were more popular among their countrymen, but he did keep some kind of semblance of order over the race that he came to own.

Perhaps the Tour found a successor today.

TEAM SKY'S FIRST TOUR de France began inauspiciously. Their declared intent to leave no stone unturned in the search for marginal gains, with no detail too small to matter, meant they pored over weather reports and forecasts before the prologue in Rotterdam. Believing that rain would arrive later in the day rendering the 8.9km course slower, the tactical decision was made to put Bradley Wiggins out early to miss the downpour and set a fast time.

'Too clever by half,' rued Bradley later, after he got caught in the showers that arrived earlier than expected, then watched as the hitters shot round a rapidly drying course to render his time something of an embarrassment. Seventy-seventh for a man who had finished third and fourth in the previous two Tour de France prologues he had contested was not the ideal start.

All the talk of the first week revolved around the third stage which would take the field over a big slice of the familiar *pavé* of Paris–Roubaix. After a protest-driven go-slow had ruined a rain-drenched first stage, deemed dangerous by the bunch after multiple pile-ups, this was the first opportunity for a shakedown. Brad rode with his customary aplomb over the crooked setts, and was delighted to keep a low profile in the Sky team despite a fine eighth place on the stage, as the plaudits all went to his young teammate Geraint Thomas. The youngster had blasted over the cobbles and run the cobblemeister Thor Hushovd close for the stage win, settling for second place and the white jersey of best young rider. He was second overall, too, while Brad was up to fourteenth. Not bad for the nascent team.

The race sped across northern France and down towards the Alps, Mark Cavendish taking back-to-back stage wins for HTC, the new name of the High Road set-up. A tricky *moyenne montagnes* stage in the Jura followed. Sylvain Chavanel soloed to victory while the favourites kept a close eye on each other on the climbs. Brad picked up a few places as the race shed a few non-climbers and looked forward to tackling the Alps from the comfort of eleventh on GC. The real action would begin the next day with a journey into the mountain bikers' paradise of Morzine and Les Gets, with a mountain top finish at Avoriaz.

This would be where the favourites would show their hands and we would know who was in charge of this absorbing race.

Throughout his long winning streak, the most amazing thing about Lance Armstrong was his invincibility. He never crashed. He never fell ill. He never had mechanicals. He never suffered. It was this aura of untouchability that did for his great rival Jan Ullrich more than anything else: Ullrich simply believed that Armstrong could not be beaten. His comeback had been slightly different. The previous year had ended up with a podium place, yes, but he was in effect well beaten by Alberto Contador and Andy Schleck. This race was turning into a disaster. That force field had well and truly evaporated. Firstly, a puncture on the cobbled stage had left him distanced and floundering in a dusty choke of team cars with no team assistance, chasing alone for miles and ending up with a significant deficit. Another rivet was removed from his cast-iron suit of armour on this stage to Avoriaz, when the great man actually had a crash. Then another. Then another. The only three times anybody could remember Armstrong crashing in the Tour de France – all in one day. He rolled over the line 11'45" after the winner, Andy Schleck.

Team Sky suffered in the first of those spills when they lost the excellent Simon Gerrans to a broken arm. There wasn't any good news from Bradley Wiggins to cheer the team up, either. After looking good for the majority of the day he struggled on the final climb up to Avoriaz, losing touch when the main group was still quite large. In his diaries, published as *On Tour,* he contemplated what had happened. 'Was it the heat or altitude, or have I got my training wrong?' His uncertainty was all-pervading. The British public, high on Cav's stage wins and full of expectation for Brad and the new team, were brought down to earth with a bump. Even if this was a blip, our man was now 2'45" behind the new leader, the World Champion, Cadel Evans. That was a lot of time.

After a rest day, the peloton tackled the biggest day's climbing of the Tour; 66km of the 207 were spent going up mountains, the biggest of which was the Col de la Madeleine, just before the finish in Saint-Jean-de-Maurienne. Once again, it was depressing viewing for Bradley's fans as he found himself fighting to stay in touch with the leaders. He lost the best part of five minutes to Alberto Contador and Andy Schleck, the men he had aspired to beat. It was a chastening and sad day for the hero of Athens, Beijing and Ventoux. Mick Rogers was also enduring a rough time as leader of the HTC-Columbia team, and it seemed increasingly likely that this would be the last time he would be seen as a contender in the world's biggest race.

The Tour de France quickly became the Schleck–Contador show as they put on a battle royal. Andy had lost his brother Frank as early as that Roubaix-style stage with a broken collarbone on the *pavé*, and some critics seemed to think that this actually allowed him to express himself and ride more freely, a suggestion hotly denied by the Schlecks and their Saxo Bank team.

They would rage against each other all the way to Paris, where the difference gained when Contador took advantage of Schleck's mechanical problems in the Pyrenees was all the Spanish rider needed to retain his title.

Mark Cavendish picked up an incredible five stages in the race. Brad took a quietly creditable top ten finish in the long time trial. But 24th place at the Tour de France was not what he or the team had in mind when they signed up to this great project. Many traditionalists had baulked at Team Sky's new methods. They perceived as arrogance the notion that a British team could come along and just tell them all, 'You've been doing it all wrong.' There were sniggers in the *salle du presse* at Wiggins's travails in the mountains. 'All part of the plan,' they would chuckle. Wiggins, Yates and Brailsford wanted to come back in 2011 and shove those laughs right down their throats. But they needed to find a better way of doing it.

Contador inadvertently summed up the problem when caught in a philosophical mood in Paris. 'Cycling is not like mathematics; there are moments when you are well prepared and everything runs smoothly, and there are times when you are well prepared and everything does not.'

The drawing board beckoned.

There was an unsavoury postscript to the 2010 Tour de France when it was announced at the end of September that Alberto Contador had tested positive during the race for Clenbuterol, a steroid. In one of the more convoluted drugs cases in sporting history, he fought a long battle to clear his name and eventually failed. All his results from that moment forward were expunged until his return to racing in late 2012. The record books now show that Andy Schleck won the 2010 Tour de France, but the Luxembourger would dearly love to cross the line first before his career is over. Time is on his side: he is five years younger than the 2012 champion.

STAGE 15:

Samatan–Pau, 158.5km
Monday, 16 July 2012

We're still in the Pyrenees, and will be in them or under their shadow for most of this riveting final week. A hillyish day today is followed by the now traditional second rest day, then two big days in the high mountains for Bradley Wiggins to beat off his challengers for the yellow jersey. And he has Saturday up his sleeve – the second individual time trial in this race where he will not be expected to concede anything to anybody.

Perhaps it's the looming rest day, but today's stage holds nothing of interest for the contenders. A break goes. It is brought back. Repeat. Another break goes and is chased for a while, then left to its own devices. The break rides powerfully together for a while, then attack each other to try and win the stage. When Pierrick Fédrigo storms by Christian Vande Velde to win in Pau for the second time in his career it's great for him and his FDJ team, and for the French who celebrate another stage victory. Those of us with an interest in the greater prizes on offer in this year's Tour will have to wait until after the rest day to see them unfold.

★

So. Where do you stand on Lance Armstrong? Persecuted hero? Or inveterate liar and cheat?

It's impossible to talk about cycling in 2012 without some discussion of Armstrong, his career and inevitably his alleged use of banned substances over that time. This seems particularly apt when we reach this second rest day and find ourselves facing a depressingly familiar story of a rider being accused of doping.

It's worth reacquainting ourselves with the Armstrong legend; a story such as this has never been heard in the history of sport and is equally unlikely to be repeated.

There are echoes of Bradley Wiggins's own upbringing in Armstrong's childhood in that they were both sons of an errant father and a fiercely protective and loving mother to whom they remained close. However, where Brad hides his fierce competitiveness behind a lugubrious exterior and a laid-back demeanour, Lance makes no effort to contain his combative nature. Indeed, he has used it as a bludgeon his whole life.

There was a reasonable buzz around the young Texan as soon as he turned professional with the Motorola squad in the early 1990s, such was his brashness and willingness to be an iconoclast for the new wave of English-speaking *arrivistes* sweeping away cycling's European stranglehold. He famously fell foul of the revered Italian classics legend Moreno Argentin in an early appearance in Europe seemingly for being unaware not only of the man's achievements but also the races in which he achieved them. This healthy disregard for reputation was as refreshing to see for the newcomers to the sport as it was disrespectful to those who sought to honour the old brigade.

But it wasn't until the barrel-chested 23-year-old scored an immense and unanticipated victory in the torrential autumn rain of Oslo in the 1993 World Championship Road Race that the cycling public really noticed Lance Armstrong. The swash-buckling attacking ride, the disregard for personal safety, the disregard for reputations of the old order were all there as Armstrong stormed into the rainbow jersey and declared himself a proper bike rider.

His career as a one-day great developed beautifully, with storming rides in the spring classics and Tour de France stage wins marking him out as a hot favourite for the first open Olympic Games – 1996 in Atlanta on home soil. The Olympics had been the preserve of amateur sportsmen up to this point, meaning the roll-call of champions was less than impressive, but for the first time the big guns would be there. Miguel

Indurain led the charge of the legends, becoming Olympic Time Trial Champion to add to his five Tour de France victories. Armstrong's power and savvy made him the stand-out favourite for the road race, but on the day he was strangely short on power and could only manage twelfth place behind the wily old Swiss fox, Pascal Richard.

That result may have been disappointing, but within weeks it appeared nothing short of miraculous. Still only 25, Armstrong was diagnosed with testicular cancer. The virulent disease had already spread to his abdomen, his lungs and his brain. The cycling world looked on aghast. It seemed to be a certainty. This colourful, wonderful, amazing young man was going to die.

An intensive bout of surgery and chemotherapy took place immediately and, incredibly, appeared successful, sending the cancer into complete remission.

Even from his hospital bed, his head bare from the effects of the chemotherapy and his body ravaged by the cancer, Armstrong spoke bravely of a return to racing. Scandalously, the French Cofidis team that had signed the Texan to a lucrative contract at the peak of his success sought to annul the deal. There was widespread outrage and condemnation of such a callous decision, one that still looks unfathomable twelve years later when one considers that the only reason sponsors become involved in the sport is to garner positive publicity. They may have been unwitting collaborators in the truly great part of Armstrong's story however, as his burning desire to prove Cofidis, and any other doubters, wrong drove him on and defined the rest of his career.

For Armstrong did return. Not just to his former glories but like a real-life Steve Austin, better, stronger, faster. The weight he lost during treatment was not replaced. His whole body shape post-cancer was different: slender, but just as powerful. Perhaps the pain and duress that his body had suffered also left a positive legacy. Riding up Alpe d'Huez couldn't hurt as bad as chemo. Whatever the reasons, and there were several false starts on the road back, a new Lance Armstrong emerged at the back end of 1998 with consecutive fourth places in the Vuelta a España, the World Championship Time Trial and the World Championship Road Race. His competitors had best look out.

His breathtaking and uplifting win at the 1999 Tour de France when he swept all before him was not only restorative for Armstrong, it was a Lazarus moment for the whole of cycling. On its knees after the numbing purges of 1998 when it became clear to all and sundry that drug abuse was not only common in cycling, it was endemic to such a degree that nobody was certain that there was a single 'clean' professional in the race, the Tour needed a hero. It had one now.

Forever driven onwards by his fire, which was beginning to resemble a war with the world, Lance Armstrong strung together another six wins in the world's hardest race. Yes, that's right, seven Tour de France victories. Two more than Jacques Anquetil, Eddy Merckx, Bernard Hinault or Miguel Indurain could manage. And all after rising from his deathbed. What a rider, what a man.

However, his retirement in 2005 as reigning Tour de France Champion was not met with universal regret. It wasn't just his robust dismissal of anybody who opposed him that upset public opinion, it was the constant allegations of doping that dogged him for an eternity that ground his public down. People were essentially unsure of whether they could trust in his feats.

Armstrong's surprising comeback in 2009 wasn't greeted with universal joy. It didn't go entirely to plan either. Unable to regain his former stellar level, he could only manage third in that year's Tour de France, one place above the new British hope, one Bradley Wiggins. Even though there was plenty of credit and applause inherent in that result, it was largely spoiled in the public's eyes by his attempts to unseat the winner – and clearly the strongest rider – his teammate Alberto Contador. He finished behind Contador again in his last Tour de France, this time 39 minutes adrift of the defending champion in 23rd.

Part of Armstrong, despite his stoic refusal to ever admit a mistake, must surely regret coming back to racing. His desire to prove his critics wrong overrode his diminishing powers. And it had the detrimental effect of fanning the flames still burning around his alleged use of illegal products throughout his career. He must have wished he'd stayed at home with his latest celebrity squeeze counting his yellow jerseys and resting on a *palmarès* unparalleled in the modern game.

Instead, he spent much of the time fighting a federal inquiry that ran until February 2012 before being closed down without any charges being brought. If he thought he was out of the woods though, he was wrong. Based on the testimony of former teammates, riders and associates, and on blood samples taken during the 2009 and 2010 seasons, Armstrong was charged with doping offences by the United States Anti-Doping Agency, USADA. They claimed that he had used EPO, the blood treatment that had been the scourge of 1990s cycling, and steroids, as well as illegal blood transfusions throughout his career. After initially hotly rebuffing the charges, in August Armstrong announced that he would not be contesting them. He was careful not to admit any wrongdoing, repeating his dismissal of allegations against him as a 'witch hunt', merely saying that 'there comes a point in every man's life when he has to say "enough is enough". For me, that time is now.'

USADA responded by removing those seven victories from the miscreant's possession. They gave him a lifetime ban from competition and backdated it to 1 August 1998, meaning that all his results since that date – effectively, his return to successful racing after cancer – were nullified.

To return to the question: hero or villain?

Once upon a time, many in cycling held a degree of sympathy for Armstrong's situation. Drug testing in the late 1990s and early part of this century was a mess. There was no test for synthetic erythropoietin or EPO, the drug that had transformed the endurance of many cyclists. Since it is a substance that appears naturally in the body, it was difficult to isolate. It mirrored the effects of training at altitude, something that cyclists have done since time immemorial knowing the benefits it would bring. The sympathy for Armstrong stemmed from popular opinion preventing him from using the understandable reasoning that many of his contemporaries were beginning to espouse: 'Yes, I took drugs . . . just like everybody else.'

Armstrong's self-acclaimed position as 'the most tested athlete of all time' and his proud boast that he had 'never failed a test' was sorely tried by the development of that long-awaited EPO test, because samples from his Tour wins had been preserved with such an eventuality in mind.

As more and more cyclists and ex-cyclists, often under the threat of prosecution, admitted their own involvement in what they saw as a curse of their time, Armstrong steadfastly refused to acknowledge any guilt. His return from retirement merely seemed to point out that the world had moved on, and that cycling didn't dance to the narcotics puppet master's beat any more. Lance was out of step with the cleaner new world order. He was an unwelcome reminder of a dirty past.

It won't have escaped anybody's notice that the new Tour de France Champion, inheritor of Lance Armstrong's crown, is one of this new world's most outspoken critics of the old ways.

In a recent *Guardian* article, Bradley Wiggins wrote an impassioned defence of his sport in 2012 and let those who weren't prepared to play by the rules have a piece of his mind. 'When I look back, we now have an idea of what was going on in the sport back then, and it was a different era. Personally, I used to find it difficult. You'd be trying to negotiate a contract – say, £50,000 – I had two kids to worry about, a livelihood to earn in the face of what was going on, and people beating me because they were doping. I wasn't shy of saying what I thought about doping, because it directly affected me and the lives of my family.'

Things have improved greatly via better testing. Brad himself and the reformed David Millar have made the simple, key point that it is essential to make not cheating more attractive than cheating. Writing in the same paper, the renowned cycling journalist and drugs-in-sport commentator William Fotheringham noted, 'The temptation to dope needs to be countered in the athlete's mind with "Why would I?" rather than "Why wouldn't I?"'

Brad explained that much of his long-held stance against doping stemmed from cultural differences. In the cycling heartlands of other European countries people can pick up a ban or be implicated in a scandal, sit tight for a few months and return unscathed. At a recent visit to a cycling clothing company in Italy, it was truly astounding to see one framed picture or jersey or medal of a cycling star brought down by their unmasking as a fraud, still revered and lauded as heroes in the trophy room.

In Britain, it's just plain cheating and you'd better have a bloody good story to get out of that. David Millar's post-drugs-bust career has been defined by his need to point out that he is a cheat, that he did wrong and he knows it, which is to be applauded. These lines in the first pages of his autobiography are eye-wateringly frank: 'My name is David Millar. I am a professional cyclist, an Olympic athlete, a Tour de France star, a world champion – and a drugs cheat.'

As Brad wrote in the *Guardian*, 'If I doped I would potentially stand to lose everything. It's a long list. My reputation, my livelihood, my marriage, my family, my house. Everything I have achieved, my Olympic medals, my world titles, the CBE I was given. I would have to take my children to the school gates in a small Lancashire village with everyone looking at me, knowing I had cheated, knowing I had, perhaps, won the Tour de France, but then been caught.'

Wiggins's article was by way of explanation for his comments a few days prior when, wearied by the day's tribulations that were barely over, he responded robustly to a question on his own legitimacy regarding drug use, by labelling those who suspect him of foul play as 'just fucking wankers. I cannot be doing with people like that. It's easy for them to sit under a pseudonym on Twitter and that sort of shit rather than getting off their arses in their own lives and apply themselves and work hard at something and achieve something. And that's ultimately it. Cunts.'

For every person outraged at his 'foul-mouthed rant' there were many more who stood up and praised his forthright attitude to those who sought to undermine his achievements. The *Guardian* column was thankfully free of an apology. It was a succinct and reasonable explanation made with more time to think through his words. While there are those within the organisation at Team Sky who may well have their hearts in their mouths every time Brad is asked his opinion on something contentious, especially when the sweat of 200km is yet to dry on his sideburns, the majority of those listening find his willingness to speak his mind a breath of fresh air. Sports reporting has already scared footballers into speaking almost entirely in clichés and platitudes that are impossible to spin into a 'rant' or an 'amazing attack'. Thank God for Bradley Wiggins and long may he continue to tell us what he thinks. After all, it's our choice whether we agree with him or not, just his decision to say it.

★

This is a race light on big names in the absence of Lance Armstrong, Andy Schleck and Alberto Contador. When the drug police discover a banned substance in the urine sample of Frank Schleck, there is a massive feeling of disappointment across the whole race. Naturally, he denies it. Naturally, he says he must have been 'poisoned'. Let's hope he is right. There must surely one day be an instance of a cyclist being wrongly accused of doping: let's hope it's today, eh Frank?

It's the second doping infringement of the race after the earlier expulsion of Cofidis also-ran Rémy Di Gregorio. Unlike Bradley Wiggins's Tour experience with Cofidis in 2007, this time Di Gregorio's team decided to stay in the race. A sign of this being a more isolated incident than the old days, or shamefully turning a blind eye? Teams have to make their own decisions in circumstances like these.

That doping stories are still likely to come out at some point in the Tour de France is depressingly predictable, but it can't shake the belief that this is a new environment. Sean Yates affirms what we've heard elsewhere. 'It's a different world these days,' he replies with a smile when asked about the prevalence of doping compared to his days as a rider. 'The cheats get caught. Catch all the cheats, and there's no cheats left.'

Frank Schleck is removed from the Tour de France by his RadioShack-Nissan team in order to 'prepare his defence'. The popular Luxembourger has lost a legion of fans overnight, especially in Britain, as Wiggins and Millar both recognise. He's also managed to bring shame and doubt upon his brother's great achievements, just by association.

Wiggins would assert that this is a position that he will never, ever find himself in. 'If I felt I had to take drugs, I would rather stop tomorrow, go and ride club 10-mile time trials, ride to the café on Sundays, and work in Tesco stacking shelves.'

Terry Leahy shouldn't hold his breath.

BRADLEY WIGGINS SEEMED TO benefit from his experience at the Tour de France in 2010. He was aware that part of his problem had been an increased propensity to fret. He went back to the old mantra of controlling the controllables. Stick to the basics. Train hard. Stay thin.

Team Sky was also strengthened. Brad had always felt at home amongst familiar faces, but now there was renewed quality, too. Edvald Boasson Hagen was still there, as was the burgeoning talent of Geraint Thomas. Their big winter signing was Mick Rogers. The experienced and popular Australian was drafted in from HTC-Columbia with the express brief of helping Brad to win the Tour. Rogers had been a team leader in his own right for some years, always with the same squad since its T-Mobile days. He felt that it was time to realign his personal goals and came to Team Sky, a set-up he had been admiring from afar throughout 2010.

A ninth place in the 2006 Tour de France and three back-to-back world time trial titles would have you think that Rogers was a veteran, but in actual fact he was only a few months older than Brad. He had also ridden poorly at the 2010 Tour, but had come to the conclusion that his days as a contender were behind him and he would be better suited to using his intelligence and steady speed to help a team in a more all-round capacity. Sadly, that wasn't going to be in 2011, as the glandular fever that had plagued him earlier in his career returned to put him out for a while. Brad would benefit massively from Mick's arrival, but not yet.

Instead, Bradley went to Paris–Nice to begin his European season and came away with third overall behind the German duo of Tony Martin and Andreas Klöden to prove that he was in hot form. The result was forged upon a narrow loss to Martin in the race's time trial which shaped the rest of the race. He was pleased with his performance: he was not expecting to be setting the world alight in March, it was July Team Sky were interested in.

To that end, there was to be less racing in 2011 and more training. The team wanted to control Bradley's form, not batter it, so this time, they rejected a ride at the Giro d'Italia and looked instead at the Critérium du Dauphiné as the ideal preparation.

The race could not have gone better. Third spot behind the big Dutchman Lars Boom in the prologue was an ideal foundation, then he and Edvald Boasson Hagen had kept pace with the climbers as the race ramped up. He was second again to Tony Martin in the Stage 3 time trial, but his superior climbing form saw Brad slip into the yellow jersey. It looked good. Sky rode strongly and intelligently to protect his lead over the remaining four stages over plenty of high passes in the Alps. The technique of staying calm and not responding immediately to everything was honed over this week, especially on the final climb to La Toussuire, when they resisted enormous pressure from Cadel Evans, Alexandre Vinokourov and Jurgen Van Den Broeck. Rigoberto Urán Urán in particular was proving a useful henchman to have.

Emboldened by their sublime team performance and the biggest win in Team Sky's short history, Yates and Brailsford resolved to take the same squad to the Tour de France in three weeks' time.

Meanwhile, Bradley nipped back to England and claimed a proud win. It was his first National Road Race title, won in great style in a Team Sky clean sweep on a Northumberland circuit. It meant that he would be going into the Tour de France resplendent in the white jersey with red and blue bands of GB Champion. He looked particularly proud whenever he raced in it: it could have been designed with the mod in mind. As well as displays by other riders like Sean Yates in that national jersey over the years, it brought to mind Olympic greats like Daley Thompson, Steve Ovett and Steve Redgrave. Right up Brad's street, in fact. It was going to be a great Tour.

There was no prologue. Instead, a tough road stage was followed by a shortish team time trial won by Garmin-Cervelo, just four seconds ahead of Evans's BMC, Team Sky and the Schleck brothers' Leopard-Trek teams, all on 24'52". The only loser in the first couple of days was defending champion Alberto Contador, who lost time after a crash on the first stage and then a few more seconds with his Saxo Bank team's performance in the TTT. Evans took a great win on the steep little Mur de Bretagne to take Stage 4, with Brad not far behind, and the race moved on, everybody doing their best to avoid the crashes that were punctuating a horrible first week. Cav took his first win of the race the next day and railed against the organisers about how dangerous the route was, after a day in which numerous crashes disturbed the action. Christophe Kern, Janez Brajkovič and Tom Boonen all made early exits with injuries. Contador was down again. These tumbles could decide the fate of the Tour, surely not what the organisers intended. It was getting silly.

Team Sky kept Brad towards the front at all times, to the extent that he ended up with a top twenty placing on Cav's stage, but it was no guarantee of safety.

The sixth stage was memorable. This was the day that Team Sky would put it all together. Edvald Boasson Hagen made Dave Brailsford a proud man by winning the uphill sprint into Lisieux after a perfect lead-out from Geraint Thomas. 'He deserves to be the first guy to win a stage in a grand tour for the team, because he's performed so well since he joined,' said the boss. Brad hadn't put a foot wrong, sitting in sixth place, ten seconds off the leader Thor Hushovd, and the team was purring like a well-tuned V8.

Twenty-four hours later, it was all in tatters. With 40km to go before the finish in Châteauroux, Brad came down heavily in a big crash at the centre of the bunch. As the road narrowed there was a squeeze, wheels touched and many riders were left with nowhere to go. The GB Champion's left shoulder hit the tarmac hard, too hard for his collarbone, which broke. The perennial broken bone for any cyclist, the collarbone was just not designed to withstand falling off bicycles. Edvald Boasson Hagen, Xabier Zandio and Juan Antonio Flecha waited anxiously for their leader, but the game was up. They were waved on, and Brad was ushered into an ambulance.

It seemed that the dream was over again. Not through bad form or bad preparation, but bad luck. Perhaps the Tour de France just wasn't for Bradley Wiggins. Perhaps that fourth place was a fluke after all, never to be bettered; a great story for the kids, but not the portent of something even greater.

The new focused Wiggins thought this was unlikely. He was sure he could win this race now.

Pau–Bagnères-de-Luchon, 197km
Wednesday, 18 July 2012

Bradley Wiggins is getting used to this yellow jersey. He's been wearing it for ten days now, long enough to look more at home in it than he did in his Team Sky kit. That cool jersey bearing the legend 'Wiggo' along its flanks, the 'O' discarded in favour of the mod RAF symbol, is something of a distant memory. The other riders get Porte, Rogers, Eisel. Brad gets a nickname.

There are stars who are well known enough to be known by their surnames: Lennon, Connery, Cobain. Then there are those big enough to be recognised by purely a colloquial shortening of their full names: Wills, Wiggo, Becks. On the rung above those are celebrities known purely by their first names: Elvis, Marilyn.

Wiggo T-shirts are beginning to appear upon the chests of Great Britain, the 'O' supplanted in the same way as the man's Team Sky jersey. Joke shops are selling out of fake sideburns. Something is happening in a country hungry for the Olympics to begin, a sporting tension and excitement that is seeing a nation's appetite for summer success whetted by the Divine Sideburns. Some have even begun to refer to Bradley Wiggins as the Modfather, surely an error as this epithet is already well and truly wrapped around the shoulders of one of his own idols, Paul Weller.

Team Sky have played their hand masterfully in this Tour so far. The lessons of 2010 and 2011 have been learned well. The direction of Brailsford, Yates, Ellingworth, Kerrison and everybody else from the Murdochs down has put the team in a golden position, and the riders have each, to a man, played their part. Wiggins holds the nap hand.

Today is the day when the cards are laid down.

When the route for this Tour de France was announced on a cold Paris day seven or so months ago, the organisers had made it clear that they expected Wednesday 18 July to be a pivotal day in the race's destiny.

In the distant historic days of Tour legend, days when the race passed over the classic quartet of Pyrenean passes were virtually *de rigueur*. Historically and hysterically dubbed 'The Circle of Death' – they're not even in a circle – the Col d'Aubisque, the Col du Tourmalet, the Col d'Aspin and the Col de Peyresourde are arranged in such a perfect geographical way that the temptation to take a race over them in succession is almost too much to bear. In recent times though, that is exactly what the organisers have managed to resist, with all the passes featuring regularly, but rarely together like this. In mitigation of the difficulty, the more common mountain top finish of a key Pyrenean stage has been foregone. Instead the natural ending in Bagnères-de-Luchon at the bottom of the Peyresourde will host *les arrivées*.

If Nibali, Van Den Broeck, Evans or, whisper it, Chris Froome have designs on winning this race, today will have figured high on their lists of launch pads for some time.

Bradley Wiggins not only knows this, he has his own ambitions to fulfil. He has said plainly that each day is a step towards Paris, and there will only be four paces left after today. And none of those will be as gigantic a stride as this one will be.

It's hot today. Not ideal for anyone in the high mountains, especially not a skinny pasty-faced Londoner.

Today there is little urge to chase any breakaways, with Team Sky unthreatened by any rider outside of the top ten. Andreas Klöden in eleventh spot is nearly ten minutes behind Brad overall, so there is no urgency to hunt down a move. Every Team Sky rider has very specific instructions for this stage, and it won't be until later this afternoon that their trial will properly begin. Thus it is no great shakes when a massive breakaway move forms early after the roll out from Pau, with virtually all the teams represented by at least one rider. Except Team Sky, of course. Both their cars trundle comfortably along behind the main field.

There are 38 riders up the road from the yellow jersey group, the best placed being Egoi Martínez, holding down eighteenth place overall and the same number of minutes behind Bradley Wiggins.

Over the Aubisque and the Tourmalet – in theory harder climbs than their smaller sisters the Aspin and Peyresourde, but further from the finish – it is Christian Knees and Edvald Boasson Hagen that perform the donkey work for Team Sky and the rest of the race.

It is Thomas Voeckler, chasing points for the King of the Mountains competition in the lead group who takes the Jacques Goddet prize for being the first man over the highest point of the Tour, this year, the Col du Tourmalet. The Pyrenees have long held an inferiority complex about their status of being lower than the Alps, and there has long been talk of surfacing the track that leads upwards from the summit of the Col all the way to the summit of the Pic du Midi above it. This would be a finish of 2,877m above sea level, another 700m higher than the Tourmalet. The gradient of the road and the accusations of spectacle-over-sport that would follow such an inclusion have dissuaded the race organisers up until now. They regularly make sure that there are no super-high passes in the Alps included in the route – no Galibier in 2012 – to ensure the Pyrenees get to host the Prix Jacques Goddet occasionally.

The Tourmalet drops down into the famous Tour de France village of Sainte-Marie-de-Campan, where blond Pyrenean cattle roam carefree across the common that marks the beginning of the Col d'Aspin. Today, we're trekking up the thickly wooded western shoulder, giving the riders some respite from the July temperature.

Liquigas-Cannondale show their hand. The entire luminous-green squad gather at the front to lift the pace. Team Sky slip in behind them, confident that it will be their other rivals who feel the pain. *Domestiques* don't come with much better

CVs than Ivan Basso, and the former Giro d'Italia Champion ratchets the hurt up another notch to stretch the line behind him to breaking point. His leader Vincenzo Nibali is confident enough to call upon the full power of his team and to demonstrate again that he's not scared of Wiggins or Team Sky.

But, as Team Sky had wagered, it is not the British team that is suffering. The casualty is the champion, Cadel Evans. This time his BMC team are there in number unlike his horrible isolation at La Planche des Belles Filles eleven days ago, but they are unable to prevent him from losing contact with the Liquigas-Cannondale-driven group. Worryingly for the Australian and his team, there is still a full 50km left to race, another first category mountain, and then hammer it well and truly down at the front.

Out of the trees and on to the beautiful gorse-covered moorland over the Aspin, Evans is a minute behind Nibali and Evans, but a concerted pursuit around the hairpins brings him back as they fly through Arreau and over the confluence of the Nestes. He must be dreading the last climb, the long drag of the Peyresourde. Already tested beyond his limit, he must deal with Wiggins and the Team Sky dark army as well as the determination of Basso and Nibali's Liquigas-Cannondale.

Basso lifts the tempo once again, and pop goes Evans. Within minutes the group is like a bowl of Rice Krispies as Van Den Broeck, van Garderen and Zubeldia all crackle and follow Evans out of the rear. Now Nibali takes up the reins. It's what he came here to do, hurt the big names and try his best to win this Tour de France in the mountains. It's a ferocious move and the field shreds behind him. Only two men remain in pursuit of the bold Italian.

Unfortunately for Nibali, they are the only two men above him on the GC and they are the Team Sky teammates Chris Froome and Bradley Wiggins. Froome takes up the effort smoothly, the loyal lieutenant once again to his leader Wiggins, pacing the yellow jersey inexorably back on to Nibali's wheel. For all Liquigas-Cannondale's fine efforts, they have only succeeded in leaving their leader exposed against the combined might of the race's best two riders. He tries again to dump them as they close in, and this time it's the yellow jersey himself that bridges for the duo. None shall pass.

In the sort of sight beloved of Tour followers over the decades and befitting of such an epic *parcours,* the top three in the race clear the summit of the last climb together, fighting each other every pedal turn of the way.

The plunge into Bagnères-de-Luchon cannot split them and they breast the line together, seven minutes after Thomas Voeckler has celebrated another famous solo victory and claimed the treasured polka dot jersey of best climber. Cadel Evans is sadly not there with them. The tribulations of the Australian as he laboured under the combined pressure of Liquigas-Cannondale and Team Sky have left him another four minutes adrift by the line. He will not retain his crown of Tour de France Champion now, with more than eight minutes to conjure up on Wiggins from somewhere.

Sean Yates may not be saying it out loud, but he's eyeing the Team Sky one-two with Wiggins and Froome in Paris on Sunday. He tells the team's website: 'It's got to the point where whatever we say isn't doing them justice. This is no ordinary stage race. It's the Tour de France and we are into the third week now and they have been consistently amazing. Everyone is hurting in the race but it panned out really well for us today. The break went without anyone really dangerous in it so we could just ride. Liquigas-Cannondale took it up a bit in a bid to get rid of Cadel. Then Brad and Froomey had the legs to follow Nibali when he tried to get away. It was probably the toughest stage of the Tour so to come through that in the manner we have done is a great achievement for the team.'

TEAM SKY HAD A clear plan for 2012. It was pretty similar to 2011, actually, but didn't involve their leader falling off.

First, they still thought they could add to their team for the Tour. Mark Cavendish was brought in at great expense to extend the image of the British team, but the Tour line-up, especially if it was to accommodate Cavendish, would need more specialists rather than the great all-rounders like Juan Antonio Flecha and Simon Gerrans. More soldiers to ride alongside Wiggins in the mountains. In came the Australian pairing of Mick Rogers, recovered from illness, and his prodigiously talented compatriot Richie Porte. In came Kanstantsin Siutsou who had impressed them so much in last year's Dauphiné.

The plan was to keep this nucleus together all the way through the spring right up to July. Team spirit would be strong. They would understand each other's strengths and weaknesses, and they would always, but always, ride as a team. Marginal gains. Control the controllables. Team Sky were building a crack unit to win the yellow jersey and then protect it.

Their first stop was the relatively low-key Volta ao Algarve in Portugal in an effort to find some warm weather in February. Edvald Boasson Hagen and then Richie Porte both won stages and wore the leader's jersey. Porte's stage win even involved a mountain top finish, which was a pleasing way of introducing himself to his new team. True to their word, Team Sky were riding as a unit, and it was powerful front running by Bradley Wiggins and Chris Froome that had set up the Aussie's win. The week ended with Brad pipping Tony Martin to take the time trial stage and Richie Porte finishing a couple of seconds back to keep the jersey and his first overall win for Sky. Not bad for a week's work in February.

They upped sticks for a much bigger challenge in France. Paris–Nice began much as it had the year before, with Brad finishing second in the time trial. This time he was only one second behind the winner, Swedish TT specialist Gustav Erik Larsson.

Once upon a time, Brad had been caught out by crosswinds and had vowed it would never happen again. On Stage 2 of Paris–Nice the vanquished became victor, as it was he who saw the danger and led a select group away from the main field in a similar split to that day into La Grande Motte in 2009. There were still around 80km to go, but when Brad picked up two bonus seconds at the intermediate sprint with Larsson nowhere to be seen, stuck in the second or third echelon, the jersey was virtually guaranteed. Brad drove the group on almost single-handedly, catching the eye of Daniel Benson, who was there for cyclingnews.com: 'At times he would accelerate from the front, creating a gap, before soft pedalling and allowing his companions to follow him once more. This is a rider at the peak of his game and Sky's ambition of winning the Tour within five years, something they've publicly stepped back from in the last two years, now looks a distinct possibility.'

Team Sky set about controlling the race and protecting their leader's six-second lead. It didn't sound much, but was a gulf, such was Wiggins's form and the quality of his support. Alejandro Valverde tried to unseat the yellow jersey on the uphill Stage F4 finish into the Lot *bastide* town of Rodez, but Wiggins matched him without breaking stride. The pair were side by side in second and third the following day into Mende, where Vacansoleil's Lieuwe Westra pipped them both and revealed himself to be the real danger on the stiff climb to the finish.

Team Sky successfully protected his lead all the way to the final time trial, the ascent of the famous Col d'Eze above the glittering blue Mediterranean. Off last, wearing full skinsuit and time trial helmet in contrast to his less prepared rivals, Wiggins won the stage and the race, completing a thoroughly dominant performance. The nature of the win was perhaps even more important to the team than the fact that this was their biggest victory to date.

From there it was down to the Volta a Catalunya, or Catalan Week as it used to be known in English-speaking parts. When snow hit the race on the third stage, Team Sky thought it best not to risk their star's incredible form and withdrew him from the race. Brad's training plan, under the watchful eye of personal coach Tim Kerrison, was based upon training more than racing, as Brad explains: 'My coach has not been in cycling for long, he's come from swimming, so I've pretty much been training like the swimmers train. I've been constantly training through the year, so it's not like the traditional way for cycling, which is starting in January fat or in really bad condition, and then building, building and showing form in these races.'

Sean Yates, Bradley Wiggins and Richie Porte headed to Mount Teide on Tenerife for the pre-summer training camp Team Sky had planned. It would be here over a punishing few weeks they would build the climbing power needed to overcome the high Alps and Pyrenees in the Tour de France. In the old days, Brad would have been heading for Tenerife for a few days in the sun and a few beers with his mates, but that was the Brad who couldn't win the Tour de France.

At 3,718 feet, Teide is the highest point in Spain, despite the fact that it's a long way from mainland Europe. It's a perfect place for altitude training, as it's higher than virtually any European peaks and a lot dryer. It also has an amazing accommodation complex nestling in its valleys, and has become very popular with the Team Sky visitors.

By May, Bradley Wiggins had only raced three times. He'd won a stage and finished third in one of them, won a stage and won the second race outright, and abandoned the third after two days due to a blizzard.

Things were looking ominously good.

STAGE 17:

Bagnères-de-Luchon–
Peyragudes, 143.5km

Thursday, 19 July 2012

It's a rare day in modern grand tour racing when the riders are afforded the luxury of beginning a stage from the place they finished the night before. It's a particular beef of the riders not often seen by the public, but transfers between stages are probably the least popular thing about long races.

After the stage finish, when riders may be either boiling or soaking, there are a few formalities. If you have a rider in the leader's jersey, in Team Sky's case Bradley Wiggins, there will be a compulsory visit to the dope testers' wagon immediately after the finish line, which involves a fight though the scrum of ever-present photographers and journalists. There are almost 5,000 people with media accreditation on this Tour de France, and it sometimes seems that every single one of them wants to push a microphone under Brad's nose or a camera in his face at the same time.

The jersey wearers and stage winner are then presented to the crowd and to a line-up of dignitaries resembling a provincial wedding at the side of the stage. Bernard Hinault will shake hands many times and the ludicrously anachronistic podium girls will kiss a lot of sweaty pink cheeks. Then there is a wait for the rest of the team to arrive. The *autobus* group of non-climbers regularly rolls in more than half an hour behind the leaders in the mountains.

In days gone by, the riders would then squeeze into any remaining seats in the team cars and *soigneurs'* people carriers to be driven off still in their kit, aching legs bunched up under dashboards or behind the driver's seat. Being a team leader in the 1990s meant getting to sit in the front.

Then there can be a drive of anything up to a couple of hours to the hotel, which will hopefully be situated close to tomorrow's start. If only it could be close to the finish, too. With the race scheduled to finish between 4 p.m. and 4.30 p.m. each night, the traffic is often at its worst.

Hence the advent of the bus. The bigger budget teams began using the luxury coach as a means of transport in the 1990s. Teams would often have two: one a genuine coach for the riders, the other functioning as a storage unit for bikes and the mechanics' workshop.

Things went to another level in 2010 when Team Sky arrived on the scene. Now, we wouldn't want to suggest that professional cyclists are a shallow or immature bunch of folk, but there was only one topic of conversation around the peloton in the first weeks of that season – 'Have you seen the Team Sky bus?!'

As part of his legendary attention to detail and desire to make the smallest thing as good as it could possibly be, Dave Brailsford didn't just buy a bus. He hired a man from Formula One to come and design the best one possible.

Then he ordered two.

The maximum number of riders for any one race is nine, so the bus has just nine seats in the riders' cabin, affording them maximum room. The seats swivel inwards for presentations, team talks, or to watch videos on the HD screen that drops down behind the driver's seat. The chairs themselves are deep leather armchairs with a console table hidden in the armrest that becomes a plush platform for a laptop or even – imagine! – a book. There are electronically controlled leg rests, inbuilt Bose headphones and, naturally, a Sky+ TV controller.

The section behind the mood-lit riders' cabin contains the toilet and behind that the shower room with automatic frosted doors, and enough space for even Christian Knees and Ian Stannard to get their hair wet without bending over.

The rear section houses a comfortable massage area that doubles as a lounge and meeting room when not in use. It is no surprise to find a state-of-the-art coffee machine available here.

Underneath the top deck where all these features look proudly out through blacked-out glass on to the world below, a bank of washing machines and tumble driers restore dirty kit to pristine condition for the next day's efforts.

The best feature is saved until last. Picture the scene: five hours in the saddle in a rainstorm and it's virtually dark when you finally squelch into the drenched finish area and through the line. There are a thousand vehicles parked in the vicinity and you've never been to this town in your life. How do you find the sanctuary of the bus? Have no fear. The Team Sky bus has an extendable rooftop antenna with a red beacon on top to guide you home.

★

The joy of finishing and starting in the same town is the glittering jewel in a morning filled with trepidation.

'On paper, it doesn't look as bad,' says Bradley Wiggins of today's stage. Compared to yesterday, maybe, but there are still four classified climbs to scale, including the impressive Port de Balès and the Peyresourde in the opposite direction to yesterday. Perhaps most dangerous of all to Wiggins and Chris Froome is the uphill finish at Peyragudes above the mountain's peak. With such a short stage into which to cram all this activity, it's certain there will be fireworks. Vincenzo Nibali will see today as his last opportunity to unseat one or other of the Team Sky dynamic duo and his attacking style makes it unlikely that he will accept defeat lying down.

The early action on the stage concerns the fight for the climber's jersey which will be decided today. Thomas Voeckler, not content with his brace of solo stage wins, wants the polka dot jersey to take home and is locked in battle with Astana's Fredrik Kessiakoff. Voeckler took the jersey off him yesterday, but only four points separate them and Kessiakoff is determined to snatch it back. It makes for a ferocious battle over the beautiful passes of the Col de Menté and Col des Ares, then on to the formidable Port de Balès before Voeckler can truly lay claim to the jersey the whole of France is willing him to win.

It's on the Port de Balès that Liquigas-Cannondale show that they are going to make the pace again. It all starts to get a little bit uncomfortable at the sharp end of the race and the group thins quickly, but the favourites all maintain their places with the Peyresourde to come.

It's now or never as they begin to tackle the legendary slopes for the second time in two days. Riders who have been out in front of the yellow jersey group are gobbled up one after another like plankton in a whale's mouth as the peloton's relentless pace shows no sign of slowing. Lotto Belisol make their own move over the Liquigas-Cannondale and Team Sky-fronted group, as Jurgen Van Den Broeck uses his teammate Jelle Vanendert's attack as a springboard for his own move. In fourth spot overall, one can only lament ' Van Den Broeck's bad luck in the earlier part of this race when he lost crucial time to a mechanical fault: who knows what chaos he could have caused if he had been closer to Wiggins when the big mountains were reached? Similar to Nibali in his attacking mentality, having twin dangers for Team Sky to look out for could have made this a very different race.

The Lotto Belisol attack has splintered the race and created a tiny group of only eight riders. Van Den Broeck is still there, as is Vincenzo Nibali and the Team Sky duo of Bradley Wiggins and Chris Froome. Chris Horner of RadioShack-Nissan is hanging in there with the French stage winners Thibaut Pinot and Pierre Rolland. Cadel Evans hasn't made the cut, but his BMC teammate in the white jersey of best young rider Tejay van Garderen has. He now sits above his leader in fifth spot with Evans one behind and losing time.

Only the brave Alejandro Valverde remains ahead of this group from the earlier break which has led the way over today's mountains. He is just over a minute in front but beginning to labour within sniffing distance of the line.

Wiggins and Froome are cruising; the former with his back flat and high tempo spinning style, Froome more hunched but just as untroubled. They share a brief chat, gauging the state of the group around them. Wiggins senses that Nibali in particular is finding the pace hard to maintain after his Herculean efforts of the last few days. At Wiggins's instigation, Froome takes up the pace.

In a glorious moment that will remain with British cycling fans forever, the two men move clear together. Now they will win this amazing race – the Tour de France will be won by a Brit for the first time. Two of them will surely stand side by side on the podium in Paris where no man from these shores has ever stood before.

The question remains: who will be on the top step? Or even, who deserves to be on the top step? While these two great teammates have proved beyond all doubt they are the strongest two riders in this race, the argument over who is the better of the two is far from being won. With Valverde looking likely to be reeled in as the pair fly up the last slopes to Peyragudes, Wiggins begins to lose touch with Chris Froome's back wheel. Froome looks around and gestures towards Wiggins, but its meaning is difficult to decipher. Come on, Brad? Are you OK, Brad? Or, do I have to wait for you again, Brad? After a moment of daylight between them, hearts in mouths for all those watching, Froome pauses and allows his leader to rejoin him and they ride on proudly to the finish unchallenged. They arrive nineteen seconds after the ecstatic Valverde, but clear of their true rivals.

They have conquered the Alps and the Pyrenees. The leader board looks like this:

Bradley Wiggins *GB* (Team Sky)	
Chris Froome *GB* (Team Sky)	2'05"
Vincenzo Nibali *Ita* (Liquigas-Cannondale)	2'41"
Jurgen Van Den Broeck *Bel* (Lotto Belisol)	5'53"
Tejay van Garderen *USA* (BMC)	8'30"
Cadel Evans *Aus* (BMC)	9'57"
Haimar Zubeldia *Spa* (RadioShack-Nissan)	10'11"
Pierre Rolland *Fra* (Europcar)	10'17"
Janez Brajkovič *Slo* (Astana)	11'00"
Thibaut Pinot *Fra* (FDJ)	11'44"

The performance was greeted with unrestrained delight at Team Sky, but it wasn't a sentiment universally shared. Many Tour followers and fans were of the opinion that the strongest man in this race was about to finish it in second place. The exchange between the first- and second-placed riders in the final moments of the stage, allied to that memory of Froome being made to wait for Wiggins at La Toussuire, has given the theorists much to talk about.

Laurent Jalabert, former world number one and a Tour de France legend said on French TV, 'It wasn't a grand gesture. You don't do that between teammates. I think it darkens the triumph of Wiggins.'

Brad, for his part, was self-critical, explaining that a dangerous belief that the race was won had caught him in a moment's reverie: 'I heard on the radio that we were alone, just the two of us. I just lost concentration and started thinking a lot of things. In that moment all the fight went out of the window, everything to do with performance.'

Froome may well have been frustrated that their late deceleration cost him a second mountain stage victory in this Tour. With Valverde just seconds up the road he had been forced – either by instructions or by his own commitment to duty – to slow and allow the courageous but tiring Spaniard to hold on to his narrow lead.

Wiggins seems to agree with that synopsis at the finish,

when he simply says, 'Chris really wanted to win the stage today.'

So, what do you think? Who deserves to win this race? Let us assume for a moment that Team Sky had not been able to keep Chris Froome after the disappointment of last year's Vuelta and he had come into this race as a rival of Wiggins on another squad. The first thing to recognise is that it would have had to be a damn fine team to challenge the dominance that Team Sky have displayed throughout this race. Even without Froome's climbing talent, they could call upon remarkable assistance via Richie Porte and Mick Rogers et al, even without Kanstantsin Siutsou. There was no room on this team for riders like Geraint Thomas or Rigoberto Urán Urán either, both of whom would be expected to make sterling contributions to the team effort.

Or maybe Team Sky would have spent the money they'd saved on Froome on a replacement? What price for a Van Den Broeck joining their ranks? Or a Luis Leon Sanchez? Or Egoi Martínez? Or Joaquim Rodriguez?

It cannot be denied that Froome has had two moments in the mountains where he has dropped Wiggins. What is uncertain is whether he could have made those gaps stick if he had truly been a rival. One characteristic that Bradley Wiggins shares with his idol Miguel Indurain is the almost total lack of a jump, a quick acceleration to make an attack or cover one. He responds to moves by staying calm and gradually lifting his own tempo until he rides himself back into contention. Putting a bike length into him halfway up a climb is no guarantee of dropping him by the top.

Then there is the time trial. Brilliant as Froome has proved against the clock in this race, can he really be expected to make up his losses to Wiggins in this department? He would need to not just beat Brad in the mountains, he would need to cane him to ensure the losses he would be bound to sustain in the time trial would be absorbed.

Finally, and crucially, there is the experience of knowing

how to lead a team and lead a race. Bradley Wiggins has won the respect and devotion of his teammates by delivering them the victories they have grafted for at the Dauphiné, the Tour de Romandie and Paris–Nice. He has learned to soak up the pressure that dressing daily in the yellow of race leader brings to all who dare to dream of victory. And in this race he has demonstrated the wise kingship of a considerate leader in his treatment of Evans, Nibali and the whole race. Even Indurain became something of a rabbit in the headlights on his first grand tour as leader when Pedro Delgado stood aside for him in the Vuelta a España only to see the lieutenant-that-was-too-good-to-be-a-lieutenant stutter in the spotlight of responsibility.

There is, of course, another possibility. What if Froome had just decided to disobey team orders? What if he had indeed put a couple of minutes into Wiggins on La Toussuire? What then? Would Wiggins have been forced to support the new race leader, or would he have duked it out with his teammate toe-to-toe for the rest of the three weeks?

That would have been some race.

THE TOUR DE ROMANDIE at the end of April is a nice race. Well organised, as you would expect in Switzerland, good roads, decent hotels and always a strong field. Riders come here for one of two reasons: their last race to fine-tune their racing legs for the Giro d'Italia, or the first serious staging post to find out where they are on the road to the Tour de France.

Team Sky were sending the backbone of what looked like being their Tour de France selection. The unit had been together in one form or another all year in races and training blocks, but this was the first time Mark Cavendish had been brought in. Their frequently questioned decision to try and fight the Tour on two fronts through Wiggins and Cavendish was about to be tested for the first time.

Throughout the entire season leading up to July, the plan was for Brad to be raced lightly and trained hard. However, a key part of that plan was that he should always race like a leader, and the team should always race to win. They should get used to controlling races, and Brad should become comfortable with leading them and seeing off challenges.

Brad had only finished two races in 2011, and the team had won both of them, through Richie Porte in the Volta ao Algarve and through Wiggins himself at the prestigious Paris–Nice. His final stage win up the classic mountain time trial of the Col d'Eze had set pulses racing, bringing back memories of Sean Kelly and Miguel Indurain winning the same stage in their pomp. Romandie was where July really began for Team Sky.

Geraint Thomas had joined up with the team after coming back from the World Track Championships in Melbourne. He was following in Brad's footsteps by mixing up his road and track programme in an Olympic year. He was now a mainstay of that glorious team pursuit quartet who were pushing on from their title in Beijing to try to recreate that moment in London. With his programme focused purely around the Tour, Brad wouldn't be riding the track events at the Olympics, which hurt him, but a man only has one pair of hands. He would go from the Tour to the Olympic road race a week later as part of a GB team that would try to emulate their superb win in Copenhagen, giving Mark Cavendish an Olympic gold to go with his rainbow jersey. His personal Olympic target would be the time trial around Hampton Court in the few days after the road race.

Thomas had arrived fresh from Melbourne as a World Champion. The team pursuit squad had done it again, this time on the Aussies' own turf. In so doing, they had even broken their own world record set on that golden night in Beijing four years ago. 'It was a great race,' said the returning Thomas. 'It reminds me of Manchester back in 2008, before the Games.

We broke the world record there, as well. I think we made a lot of gains after that and I'm sure we can do the same now.'

He'd also brought home a silver medal from the madison, where he had partnered up with Team Sky's 'other' British sprinter, Ben Swift. The aptly named Swift's opportunities had been limited more than most by the signing of Mark Cavendish and he was eager to prove himself wherever he could. A medal at the Worlds could do him no harm.

It was no surprise, against this backdrop, when Geraint Thomas won the extremely short opening prologue at the Tour de Romandie. It was even shorter than a pursuit, and he'd just become a World Champion in that. He'd beaten defending Romandie champion Cadel Evans and his own leader Bradley Wiggins who were both bothered by late rain. It does seem to follow Brad around at times. Thomas wasn't about to have his win and subsequent yellow jersey pushed aside for that, though: 'There was only really one corner. There's only so much time you can lose in one corner.'

Team Sky rode to protect the jersey on the 184km first stage, but Thomas with his track miles was not expected to compete. He was dropped on one of the hills as the climbers began to stretch their legs, and so was Cavendish. Wiggins then had a puncture as the pace hotted up with 20km to go. The bunch was flying to ensure the distanced sprinters didn't make it back up for the finish, but the adrenaline coursing through his veins not only saw Brad back up to the bunch, but carried him right up to the front.

We've seen Bradley Wiggins leading out teammates for bunch sprints before, but we haven't seen him win one. Actually, he won this stage with something akin to a lead-out, putting his head down and driving for the line from a long way out, but nobody had the speed to come round him. It was quite a moment. 'It's really nice to win a sprint like this because normally I only ever really win time trials.'

It can be hard to make significant time gaps in one-week stage races like Romandie, so organisers often spice up the racing by offering bonus seconds for stage wins. These handy seconds meant the jersey passed from Thomas to Brad, and the team could concentrate on riding like race leaders.

Those time bonuses were an issue, though. They couldn't rely on just holding the race together, and Luis Leon Sanchez demonstrated the problem by winning the third stage and moving to within one second of Brad on GC, even though Brad had finished in the same group. Victory the next day would give him the lead, and that's exactly what happened. Brad would have to dig deep if he really wanted that jersey back.

The last stage was a time trial. Now, this might be Brad's speciality, but Sanchez is the Spanish National Champion and a serial Worlds contender against the clock. It would be no walk in the park.

It was, in fact, a very fast blast. Brad took a sizeable 1'23" out of Sanchez over just 16.5km to claim the stage and the race overall. Brad's wingmen Richie Porte and Michael Rogers finished in fourth and fifth to remind everybody just what a good team this was. Team Sky in its third year was a different proposition to the Mk 1 version.

The final test before the Tour would again be the Critérium du Dauphiné. With two stage race victories under his belt, a third would complete a remarkable spring and be the perfect springboard for July. The Dauphiné's Alpine climbs would be a true indicator of the whole team's form and readiness for the big one.

Brad was second in the prologue, a second behind Australian prodigy Jack Bobridge, and professed himself happy. He certainly looked happy. He was relaxed and chatty, and not at all the frowning unapproachable Brad of 2010. As with his track career, confidence is the means through which Brad finds his true self and fulfils his ability. There was a lot to be confident about.

Cadel Evans won the first stage, a 187km trawl over six categorised climbs, but Brad took over the leader's jersey by virtue of his superior prologue. These two were shaping up to be the main rivals, not just here, but in the main event in July, too.

After a couple of inconclusive stages, one of them won by the team's ever popular Edvald Boasson Hagen, the real meat of the race lay in the long time trial. Not only was it likely to prove conclusive, it was over the same roads that the Tour de France's individual test would use six weeks later. Juicy. In that light, Brad taking half a minute out of World Champion Tony Martin was delicious, but 1'34" out of Cadel Evans was the cherry on top. Mick Rogers also moved above Evans in the overall standings. With the addition of the rapidly improving Chris Froome, Sky had three men in the top ten and had won two stages with three to go. They weren't going to be easy, though.

Meanwhile, another favourite for Paris, Andy Schleck, was having a torrid time. Losing time chunks on the early stages, the skinny Luxembourger was literally blown off his bike by the buffeting winds outside Bourg-en-Bresse and was struggling to complete the race. It had been a miserable spring all round for him, but he had come into the Tour with poor form before and ridden himself in. He would remain a favourite.

Team Sky overcame a combined attack by Evans and Vincenzo Nibali over the Col du Grand Colombier the following day, refusing to panic and grinding back up to the break, the team effort led by Wiggins himself.

The leader was profoundly immovable on the next day's massive stage, six climbs culminating in the feared Col de Joux Plane. Attacks came and went but Sky and Wiggins were imperious. The yellow jersey rode tempo the whole way, surrounded by Chris Froome, Mick Rogers and Richie Porte. All four Sky riders had taken up residence in the top ten. The others were going to have to get used to this. Of his Tour rivals, Evans was aggressive but ultimately neutralised, Nibali distanced, and Andy Schleck abandoned 60km in. Perhaps his tour dreams were looking a bit over ambitious, after all.

Team Sky controlled the last stage, too, another mountainous ride, fighting off more attempted attacks from the aggressive Evans without ever coming under sustained pressure. At the end the top four riders on GC were Wiggins, Rogers, Evans and Froome. A job extremely well executed.

'We controlled it today and have done throughout the race,' said a satisfied Sean Yates. 'I think we can be very happy with ourselves.'

Questioned again on whether Wiggins had peaked too soon – the same question was asked after every show of strength all season – Yates gave some insight into Brad's condition.

'I think that what people don't understand is that Bradley is a fantastic athlete and he's not reached his peak yet. He's not trained so hard that he's going to be exhausted. He's just training normally, but he's getting better and better. He's not trying to attain his pinnacle right now.'

That's not what Bradley Wiggins's rivals would have wanted to hear. His next race would be the Tour de France.

Blagnac–Brive-la-Gaillarde, 222.5km
Friday, 20 July 2012

The last road stage before the dash around the Champs-Élysées on Sunday is through the stunning rolling countryside north of Toulouse through Lot and the Dordogne. With the time gaps settled between the leaders and no great climbs of note, only tomorrow's test against the clock will provide any opportunity for a reordering of the classification in this year's race. Peter Sagan has had the green jersey stitched up for a while thanks to his storming stage wins and muscle-flexing performances on the hillier stages. Thomas Voeckler has secured the polka dot jersey following an epic Pyrenean shootout with Fredrik Kessiakoff. The white jersey of best young rider is safely in the hands of Tejay van Garderen.

With the sprinters thinking about Sunday, this is the archetypal dead stage. A long day in the sun for rolling along and chatting, pulling faces for the TV cameras, jolly japes like riding each others' bikes or doing wheelies, riding pillion on a police motorcycle. A group will go away and end up in Brive-la-Gaillarde ten minutes ahead of the freewheeling bunch, victory going to a late lone effort by a French newcomer.

Or maybe not.

The first half of this lengthy stage goes to plan, but there are some itchy trigger fingers back in the bunch. The first team to pick up speed and start to chase the breakaways that have been pedalling earnestly is Liquigas-Cannondale, not for the beaten Nibali today, but for his teammate in the green jersey of most consistent finisher, Peter Sagan.

They are joined by the massed ranks of Orica-GreenEDGE, still looking for some scraps in their barren debut Tour de

France. Team Sky move up on the flank, the yellow jersey safe near the back of the line, but on his wheel the rainbow jersey of the World Champion.

In front of them a number of all-out desperate movers are hanging on to slim advantages for as long as possible as the peloton thunders over the road separating them to set up the big bunch sprint. David Millar, Alexandre Vinokourov, Adam Hansen and Jeremy Roy all try to maintain their lead. Even Edvald Boasson Hagen has been up the road today – history, alas, fails to record what José Luis Arrieta thinks of Team Sky allowing a rider to join a break – but has been recalled to help the chase.

The urgency to stay clear and gain a stage win is uncommonly fierce today with the knowledge that this is almost certainly the last chance that anybody but the best time triallists and fastest sprinters will have to win.

Inside the final kilometre and the bunch still haven't made contact with the very front of the race, despite speeds of up to 60kmh.

The men with the most hunger to stay clear are the Irishman Nicholas Roche, who has grown stronger with every day in the mountains, and the serial break specialist, Luis Leon Sanchez. Holding their nerve in front of the wave like fishermen untying their boats in the face of an approaching tsunami, Sanchez manoeuvres Roche in front of him and prepares for the sprint.

Like a frantic game of speed chess, the bunch are trying to catch the escapees and line up their sprinters for the finale all at the same time.

It's the yellow jersey himself, the man who should really be taking things easy with an eye on Sunday, who leads the hunt. He hits the front of the bunch flat out, stretching the whole race behind him. On his wheel is Edvald Boasson Hagen and on his, Mark Cavendish. They mop up remnants of the break every few yards, but the line won't come soon enough for Wiggins to catch Roche or Sanchez, as the latter begins his move around the Irish rider and prepares to take his second stage of the race.

Mark Cavendish simply can't allow that to happen. Earlier than he would have chosen, he explodes from Boasson Hagen's wheel, hurtling down the finishing straight. In the last yards before his victory is complete, Sanchez suddenly looks over to his right with an expression of pure horror as Cav careers by to score one of the more celebrated of his 22 Tour de France stage wins. Nicholas Roche has the shocked look of a man who was standing too close to the platform edge when the express train came through. Matt Goss follows Cavendish through for yet another placing, pursued by Sagan's green jersey.

They were so close to the line when they were caught that Luis Leon Sanchez and Nicholas Roche are fourth and fifth respectively, in amongst the sprint.

There has rarely been a happier winner of a Tour de France stage, amazing when one considers how many Cavendish has trousered over the past few seasons. 'I haven't done nothing this Tour, so I've saved so much energy. I knew I'd be able to go long today and nobody would be able to pass me.

'We were on the bus this morning and Sean [Yates] said, "OK, it's just going to be an easy day today," and I just stuck my hand up and said, "*Pleeeease*, just give me a chance!" Brad committed straight in, Froomey committed straight in, Mick committed straight in, and the guys were like, "OK, we're going to make it a sprint today." I'm so, so happy.'

'He's the fastest man in the world, there's no doubt,' said a satisfied Bradley Wiggins. 'You saw that today with how far out he went, 600m or something, and left them for dead. I've always wanted to do that for him.'

CYCLING WATCHERS HAVE ALWAYS noticed Bradley Wiggins's individuality and style. Like many young men who spend their time in sports teams from an early age, cyclists often have a heightened sense of clothes, fashion, and what they think is cool; it's all part of the arrested development bubble of being a professional sportsmen. Brad wasn't like that though. It wasn't a case of him following the others; he was interested in other stuff. It marked him out.

As far back as his Linda McCartney days in 2001, Brad was pinning up posters of *Quadrophenia* and watching tapes of *The Sweeney*, immersing himself in 1960s and 1970s London culture. People often dismiss such things with a casual wave of 'Before my time, mate,' without realising that their own culture didn't suddenly begin the day they were born. It's been developing for decades, even centuries. Hitler was before most of our times, but that doesn't mean we don't know he was a bastard.

What it does take, to immerse yourself in a culture that began before you were born, is some form of interest. To want to know, to want to find out. For some people, it would be, say, birds or flowers. They'll hungrily read up on everything out there so they can identify a red kite or a harebell when they see one. For others it might be history, wanting to know why Henry VIII dissolved the monasteries or Germany invaded Poland. It's the sign of a fertile mind; somebody who wants to understand stuff, not just sit and wait for the world to happen to them. For those people, the world rarely does happen.

Brad was interesting. He grew his hair sometimes. He often had sideburns that wafted out from around his helmet straps. He wouldn't dream of riding for a team that expected him to wear glasses made by anyone other than Oakley.

Over the last three weeks, he had become, at the risk of hyperbole, something of a British style icon. The hair and the sideburns, yes, but more than that. The personalisation of his Team Sky kit, with 'Wiggo' along the side, the 'O' an RAF roundel. The same mod roundel on the front of his time trial helmet. These were the cool adaptations. There were also his off-bike appearances, the Fred Perry shirts with the top button done up, the adulation of Paul Weller and Pete Townshend.

Cultural expert Stuart Clapp has followed Bradley Wiggins's rise from interesting cyclist to national style icon with keen interest. 'Bradley transcends his sport, definitely. That's unusual. When pop stars are tweeting, "How cool is Bradley Wiggins?" you know he's made an impression. Pop stars want to be him, he wants to be a pop star, and he is. A popular star.

'For instance,' he continues, 'the general public emulate David Beckham's haircuts, like they're now doing with Brad's 'burns. But with Bradley, his fashion comes from a place of knowing, of being out there and living it. Beckham, for want of a better example, is dressed by a stylist. Bradley *is* a stylist.'

It's not just because he's a big star that people emulate Brad or talk about him. It's because he is cool. When Miguel Indurain was the glittering star in cycling's firmament, people didn't suddenly start growing monobrows. Lance Armstrong's Livestrong yellow wristbands are probably the only cultural impact that cyclists have made upon the public consciousness in recent years, and while they were a truly brilliant innovation, the wearing of the band indicated commitment to a cause rather than an attempt to create a style.

Other cyclists are stylish people, but that doesn't make them style leaders. As Stuart points out, 'Mark Cavendish is another huge cycling star, but no one is emulating his "steeze". That's not to say he's not well turned out, and I'm sure Dior, Gucci and Prada are delighted to have him as a customer.'

It's Brad's multi-layered character that makes him fascinating, especially compared to the footballers who are paraded through the middle pages of the tabloids on a daily basis.

'Sportsmen and women are usually pretty one-dimensional. Brad gives the papers something more than the obvious; he gives the media an angle. The whole mod thing being quintessentially British has helped, too, very well timed with it being an Olympic year. How many other sports people align themselves so strongly with a movement or fashion like that? If you can think of one, I'd like to meet him or her.

'The closest thing I can think of in terms of sport and fashion influencing each other is in skateboarding or surfing. It's different though, because those are movements rather than sports; plenty of people are in surfing or skating purely because of the fashion. And most skaters would be outraged to be described as "sportsmen". British skateboarder Geoff Rowley is a fashion icon for skaters, but they wouldn't be able to roll off a list of events he has won. Similarly, you're unlikely to ride a bike just because you like The Who.'

Brad is also riding the crest of a cultural wave when it comes to cycling due to its rapidly expanding popularity. The Middle Aged Men In Lycra, or mamils, who keep bike shops roaring through the economic depression and clog up the lanes of Britain every Sunday morning, are desperate to distance themselves from the traditional view of the cyclist in baggy tights and trouser clips, clipboards and saddle bags. They want to be cool. They want to be Brad.

And then there's his love of music. Printing his Tour play list in his published diaries. His regular tweets about music and the bands he loves, his association with the Moons and the High Numbers.

'It's nice to see a sports personality giving a shit about the arts full stop,' says Stuart. 'Mod culture is pretty well documented. The music, the scooters, the clothes. Bradley endorsing the band the Moons is pretty interesting. He was tweeting the launch of their album and I know people will buy it as a result.'

The genuine nature of Brad's passion for it all is clear, too. 'People can smell fakery a mile off with this stuff. There are enough real mods out there to sniff him out if he'd just got on to it and thought, "Ooh, mods, that's cool, I'll do that." It's not like he's gone out and bought *The Best of The Who* and a pair of desert boots and, bang, he's a mod quicker than you can shout "Bell Boy!"'

His guitar playing is well known, but it's not showy; it's for his own entertainment. As of yet, we haven't seen Bradley Wiggins and the Yellow Jerseys popping up on GMTV trying to punt out a faux northern soul record for Christmas. He's a good guitarist, too, and his choice of instruments shows a profound understanding of what's cool: a Jimi Hendrix Strat, an ES335 and, coolest of all, a Gibson Firebird. These aren't the guitars that kids learning to play buy, or grown men twiddling Metallica solos in their bedrooms have an eye for. These guitars are too cool for that. Brad understands that there's no point in visiting guitar shops that sell new instruments, as all the best guitars have already been made.

Brad's willingness to put his money where his mouth is and tell us what he cares about marks him out, but it's also a reflection of our age and the usefulness of social media in telling people stuff. Perhaps Jimmy Connors was a massive Electric Light Orchestra fan, or maybe Geoffrey Boycott travelled Europe in the winter collecting sightings of new experimental aeroplanes. 'Do you know who Jimmy Floyd Hasselbaink's favourite band was?' asks Stuart. 'Do you know which song David Gower used to get psyched-up to before he went to the popping crease? No, very unlikely, but with Bradley, people watching from afar will probably have an idea.'

The tweet that captured the public imagination the most, and really marked Bradley Wiggins out as a folk hero, didn't come until after most people were already aware of him. In fact, it may never have happened – many denounced it as fake – but the sentiment is pure Brad, and sums up perfectly why we love him so much. We want it to be true even if it isn't.

Piers Morgan, somehow a popular figure in our great nation, tweeted: 'I was very disappointed @bradwiggins didn't sing the anthem either. Show some respect to our Monarch please!'

Wiggins replied: '@piersmorgan I was disappointed when you didn't go to jail for insider dealing or phone hacking, but you know, each to his own.'

Bonneval–Chartres, Time Trial, 53.5km
Saturday, 21 July 2012

Despite the looming prospect of a Team Sky British one-two in Paris tomorrow, despite the team's great display of unity in delivering Mark Cavendish's second win of the race yesterday and despite their utter dominance of this year's Tour de France, there is still an undercurrent around the Team Sky camp.

Sluggishly, the British tabloids have picked up on the Twitter row surrounding Cath Wiggins and Michelle Cound, with the *Daily Mail* running the 'Wag War' story that had enflamed the central part of the race. Team Sky had probably hoped and even assumed that it would blow over after the team and the duo's storming procession through the Pyrenees, but it seems that Chris Froome's girlfriend is still not happy about her man being forced to play second fiddle to his leader, as she sees it.

On the day that Cavendish was the goal scorer for the team's sweeping set piece move, Cound tweeted, 'Team work is also about giving the people around you, that support you, a chance to shine in their own right.'

The inflammatory comment was quickly deleted, but not before the *Independent* had picked up on it and the whole Wiggins versus Froome rivalry, so carefully deconstructed by Team Sky, was back at the top of the agenda.

One assumes that she had in mind the top of Peyragudes on Thursday when her boyfriend had decided to wait for/ encouraged his friend and leader/was forced by team instructions to stop attacking (delete as per your choice) Bradley Wiggins near the summit of that last climb.

The time trial is so often referred to glibly as 'the race of truth' that we forget the real meaning of the cliché. It means that one can't hide behind team instructions, assistance or circumstances: it's just the man, the bike, the road and the clock. Surely, if Chris Froome wanted to demonstrate that he, and not the tall Londoner, should be the rightful leader of this race, now was the time to prove it. He wouldn't have to adhere to any plan or instructions, wouldn't be seen to attack his friend and leader, and could deliver a telling blow without any accusations of disloyalty.

Froome's motivation throughout the race has been hard to read. His performance has been exceptional and of massive assistance to Wiggins's march on Paris. The sight of Froome cruising behind Mick Rogers and Richie Porte with the yellow jersey comfortably alongside him has been an intimidating one for those who would unseat Team Sky. The fear when he has taken up the race has been tangible. Nobody could match the Kenyan-born rider when he actually led in the hills and he would have taken the King of the Mountains competition with ease if he hadn't had more pressing concerns in this race.

In his interviews he has been effusive in his praise of the team ethic at Team Sky and how everybody is expected to make sacrifices, without ever giving the impression that he wouldn't jump at a chance to win the race himself if it was at all possible. 'Anyone in a team position has to make personal sacrifices for the sake of the team, and that's what we've been doing so far, and it seems to be working for us. So, why stop doing that?'

His personal ambitions, said Froome, lay firmly at the Tour de France, but not this year. 'In my future, I might be given the opportunity to try and lead a team myself one day. But again, for now, we just need to focus on what we're doing here and achieve the goals we have here. I'm 27 at the moment, so hopefully I should still have a good ten years of racing. I do see myself as a future Tour winner, that's what I aspire to become one day.'

He walked a tightrope at times, giving an interview to *L'Équipe* that appeared to confirm that he was under some duress to continue toeing the line at Team Sky. 'I could win this Tour, but not at Sky. I cannot lie to you, it's difficult, but it's my job,' he said. 'It's a very, very great sacrifice. We have a strategy around Wiggins and everybody respects it.' He may have been suggesting that being at Team Sky meant that he was there to help Wiggins, but many commentators saw it as what tabloid football editors call a come-and-get-me plea to potential suitors.

He also made occasional references to the route of this Tour de France, possibly inferring that if it had contained more mountain top finishes and fewer time trialling kilometres – more than usual in 2012 – then he would be less happy about not being the chosen leader. When pressed on his thoughts on the 2013 race, he said, 'It all depends on the route. If there are passes, I hope Sky will be honest and all my teammates will be at my service, with the same loyalty I have shown today.' That's a hard call to make though, as Nibali and Van Den Broeck would surely applaud such a change in *parcours*, too, not to mention Alberto Contador and Andy Schleck, and he would be fighting them as much as his current skipper. And would Team Sky really ask Wiggins to support him even though he was the defending champion and a national hero? Really?

Wiggins has responded with gratitude and kind words to Froome without ever showing the deep affection that he obviously holds for Mark Cavendish, another supposed 'rival' for the support of Team Sky. The yellow jersey and rainbow jersey embraced each other in a long hug of pure joy after the latter's victory yesterday. That may have more to do with Cavendish's more emotional character though; he inspires stronger and more immediate feelings than the quieter but affable Froome. He echoed Froome's words about the future without committing himself to 2013 in quite the same way. 'Chris will have his day for sure – and I'll be there to support him every inch of the way when he does at the Tour.'

With his case to prove, Chris Froome scorches around the course of today's final time trial. The long-time leader is Luis Leon Sanchez, the National Time Trial Champion of Spain, another rider who has enjoyed this Tour de France more and more with each passing day. He would hold the lead for fully two and a half hours today as other riders came and went.

Froome's insistent style sees him set the fastest time at the first, second and final time checks out on the course, seeing off not only Sanchez but BMC's fine young emerging talent, Tejay van Garderen. The white jersey had set the best time at the first check when he arrived there a few minutes before Froome, before fading to an eventual seventh on the day. Embarrassingly, the American catches and passes his team leader Cadel Evans out of the start house one place ahead of him a minute earlier. This has not been a good race for the champion who, in contrast to Sanchez, has encountered more problems as the race has progressed. After coming into the race full of hope in the absence of Contador and Schleck Junior, the anticipated head-to-head battle with Bradley Wiggins never really materialised. However, he will leave this race with his head held high after a gutsy performance in the face of poor form and a stomach bug that has made the final week less than enjoyable. His decision to lead his team all the way to Paris when an early exit must have beckoned has won him the respect of all connected to this race, not least the winner-in-waiting, Wiggins.

Chris Froome presses all the way out into the headwind that greets him on the wide roads out of Bonneval before speeding along the narrower more protected final part of the race into Chartres, the city's bizarre lopsided cathedral spires guiding him in along the Eure. He reaches the packed finish line in a time 34 seconds less than it took Luis Leon Sanchez to cover those 53.5km. Nobody else has completed it anything like as quickly as these two and there is only one man left to arrive.

The bad news for Froome is that this last man will arrive very soon indeed.

Bradley Wiggins's languid style in the time trial is deceptive. He sits so still, his back so flat, he could be completing one of Team Sky's many wind tunnel tests designed to unearth the best equipment and position for such an event, rather than riding towards victory in the world's greatest bike race. After 14km, he is twelve seconds ahead of his teammate Chris Froome. After 30km, he has found an advantage of 54 seconds. By the finish, it is a crushing one minute and sixteen seconds difference between the two men. He has ridden this course at the cool speed of 50kph.

It is rare to see a proper victory salute in a time trial, but there are several mitigating factors in play today. Firstly, only the last man off can ever truly know if he has won a time trial. Secondly, winning a second stage in the Tour de France is a victory worth celebrating, as the demonstrative Thomas Voeckler, Peter Sagan and Mark Cavendish have all shown in the last three weeks. Becoming the first ever British winner of the Tour de France probably counts for something, too.

Bradley Wiggins stands on his pedals and thumps the air like Ayrton Senna at Monaco. The emotion so rarely seen while his face is concealed behind helmet and sunglasses is raw and available for the whole world to see. And make no mistake, the whole world is watching. Bradley Wiggins has won the Tour de France.

It is clear that the emotion had started before he even reached the finish line. 'In the last 15 to 20km I knew what my advantage was and I was thinking about my wife and kids, my mum, all of the people who've helped me get to where I am. I know it sounds cheesy, but I was thinking about the fact that I've spent my whole life working to get to this point. This is the defining moment.'

Among a host of people that have played their part in reaching that defining moment, Dave Brailsford is entitled to feel a little proprietary about the success. This whole journey began as something of a pipe dream for him and Shane Sutton, chewing the fat up on the bleachers of Manchester Velodrome years ago.

'Bradley's had an amazing race and what a way to demonstrate he is the best rider in the race by finishing with a time trial like that. I'm incredibly proud of both him and Chris as well as every single person in the team. It's never been done before by a British rider, or by a British team – it's a very special day.'

⊙

THE TWIN THREADS OF these fascinating stories were coming together. From the apartment in Ghent to the flats in Paddington. From the Hayes Bypass to Herne Hill. From the Leicester track to the velodrome in Havana. From Kuala Lumpur to Sydney. From Athens to Beijing. From an OBE to a CBE. From 78kg to 68kg. From the London *Grand Depart* to Mont Ventoux. And now from Liège to Paris. Bradley Wiggins's journey has been the stuff that dreams are made of, full of improbabilities, disappointments and unbridled success.

On the eve of his first Tour ride in 2006, Brad had said, 'I'd be gutted not to finish it. It's a race you simply have to finish. Places in the Tour are priceless so I might only ever get one chance to ride, and it's one of the few races you can look back on at the end of your career and be happy merely to have completed the course.'

Six years on and he is finishing the Tour, but not as an also-ran, as the winner.

Sir Chris Hoy and the Olympic track squad were pausing in their training each day to watch Brad's progression to Paris. The time trial in Chartres drew the loudest cheers. They knew their erstwhile teammate was going to pull off the unthinkable and be the first British winner of a race that has been run since 1903.

'The greatest achievement by any British sportsperson – ever,' was how Sir Chris described Brad's performance.

In the *Daily Mail*, Bradley Wiggins was held up as a beacon of British sportsmanship and success. David Jones wrote: 'Here is a man who inner-city children can truly relate to. He had a difficult start in life, was disinterested in school, and admits he came dangerously close to going off the rails. Instead, he got on his bike, spent countless lonely, gruelling hours developing the supreme fitness and iron willpower required to win the world's toughest race, and pedalled his way into the history books.'

The same paper reached for the book of superlatives and concentrated on one in particular: 'Ever. It certainly is a big word. Just the two syllables but huge in sport. Hugely misused, too. The best ever, the first ever. That last word is superfluous. We mean the best, we mean the first. Yet when Bradley Wiggins made his way up the Champs-Élysées, each pumping limb its own little revolution, ever has never sounded more appropriate. Bradley Wiggins is the first British winner of the Tour de France. Ever. Bradley Wiggins is the greatest British cyclist. Ever. Bradley Wiggins may well be the finest British sportsman. Ever.'

David Cameron and Nick Clegg were both apparently backing moves to knight him. Well, he already had an OBE and a CBE, and Sir Chris Hoy said he was the greatest of all time . . . Where else could they go with Brad? Intensely proud of representing his country, 'Sir Bradley Wiggins' still has an establishment ring to it that sounds awkward. But, in many ways, one can think of no more fitting accolade.

The Prime Minister, never one to miss a chance to align himself with a bit of success, said, 'I am, like everyone in the country, absolutely delighted. Bradley Wiggins has scaled one of the great heights of British sporting achievement. To be the first British person in 109 years to win the Tour de France is an immense feat of physical and mental ability and aptitude. I think the whole country wants to say, "Well done, brilliant."'

PR guru Max Clifford waded in to ensure himself some column inches by trying to assess Brad's financial worth. 'It's an amazing achievement and of course it's a great story, with his dad and all that went before. It's a real triumph out of real tragedy, and we love those kind of stories. The whole of Europe is at his feet. In the next couple of years we are talking £10 million or £20 million.'

Brad would be interested to read that, especially after his first brush with success earned him no more than a £35,000 contract to ride a bike for a year. He'd be sure to work a little bit harder to turn this one into a drop of cold hard cash for his family.

The *Independent* declared Bradley 'King of France' and noted that 'what is totally new, also, was to see a triple Olympic track champion win the Tour de France.'

The *Star* looked for a way to link the win with the Olympics that were starting in less than a week. 'Olympic chiefs were last night urged to let British Tour de France hero Bradley Wiggins light the opening ceremony cauldron. His incredible victory has sparked calls for him to be awarded a knighthood and made BBC Sports Personality of the Year. And fans demanded he be given the honour of firing up the Olympic cauldron at Friday's opening ceremony.'

Bradley himself is circumspect and relaxed. He's had a long time to think about this. 'Going back as a child, watching the Tour on telly from the age of ten, eleven, twelve, all through the Indurain years, dreaming that one day you would win the Tour,' he said at a news conference, 'but you never really think it's possible. What chance does a kid growing up in central London ever have to win the Tour?

'I'm determined to not let it change me,' he went on. 'I'm not into celebrity life or all that rubbish. So much of British culture is built around people who are famous for doing nothing. I'm still Bradley Wiggins. At the end of the day, I have to go home and clean up dog muck. At the end of the day, it's just sport. There will be more Tour winners in the future.'

Rambouillet–Paris, 120km

Sunday, 22 July 2012

'There is a set of railings, about six or eight of them, just before the entrance to the Place de la Concorde, about a kilometre from the Tour de France finish on the Champs-Élysées. I stood on those railings with my brother and my mum on 25 July 1993 watching the Tour de France go past.'

One might think that Great Britain's history, or lack of history, at this venerable old race might mean a lack of understanding of what it means: the cultural weight, the social power of the Tour de France. A country raised on dashed footballing hopes, Wimbledon near-misses, some Olympic achievements and the odd cricketing or rugby success would surely have no place in its hearts for a French national celebration?

As Bradley Wiggins so beautifully evokes in his *Guardian* column, the Tour de France means a great deal to a lot of British people. Football stadiums may be full with multitudes paying the wages of the super-rich every weekend. Millions of satellite dishes zing with the pictures beamed in from the MCG or Newlands or even Trent Bridge. Twickenham resounds not just to the roar of those inside when Chris Ashton swallow-dives over for a try, but thousands of pubs across the land. And the boundaries of Henman Hill can be redrawn to encompass the outline of this sceptred isle when Andy Murray is on Centre Court. But for more of us than most would guess, the Champs-Élysées is where our sporting hearts lie.

And it looks as though every single one of us is in Paris today.

Just like Brad, brother Ryan and mum Linda in 1993, British cycling fans have hopped on the Eurostar, driven down to the Chunnel, used up their *Sun* ferry vouchers or jetted out of Stansted to watch the arrival of the Tour on to the neat cobbles of downtown Paris. Only there's a few more now than when they were here.

The circuit around the Champs-Élysées and the Place de la Concorde is about 7km. Let's say that there is room for three people along every metre of barrier along that course. Just for fun, let's pluck a number out of the air and assume that the crowd is an average of six deep. We won't try to count the people in grandstands or hospitality areas or hanging out of hotel windows, just like we won't take into account the crowd-free bit through the tunnel. I make that, at a conservative estimate, about 126,000 people on the barriers. Another rough guess based purely on the draped Union Jacks, mod target T-shirts and fake sideburns would make about a third of them British. There must be a lot of Sunday drivers in the shires thinking, 'Where the hell are all the cyclists today?'

The Tour de France may be won for Bradley Wiggins and Team Sky, but there's still work to be done. One man has won this traditional closing stage for the last three years straight, and he'd sincerely like to make it four. His name is Mark Cavendish.

He has been able to call upon the full might of HTC or its various incarnations to lead him to those three emphatic victories, something he has acknowledged has not always been possible this year at Team Sky. Today though, there is no doubt that the entire machine will be placed at his disposal as Brailsford's boys look to end their dream race in style.

The dead corner under the Arc de Triomphe where the bunch turns back on itself to race back down the other side of the famous old boulevard ought to be renamed Hyde Park Corner for the afternoon, such is the depth and volume of the British support. Though the roars of approval are huge around the whole lap, the British riders glance up with a grin on the far side of the turn at the sheer amusement of the situation.

Nobody ever seems to win on the Champs-Élysées from a breakaway, but that doesn't stop some optimistic types from trying their luck, even if it gives them nothing more than an opportunity to show the folks back home that they're still in the race. Jens Voigt, the perennial evergreen chancer, is one of the more successful optimists and has even pulled off the odd win here and there over his fascinating nineteen-year top-level career, a couple of stages in this old race among them. If anybody can pull it off, it's him, and he's still in front of the charging bunch when they hear the bell that tells them there is only one of the eight laps of the finishing circuit remaining.

When sprinters want to win, it's hard to deny them. Team Sky are lining it out and they've got assistance from Sagan's Liquigas-Cannondale, Goss's Orica-GreenEDGE, Farrar's Garmin-Sharp and Greipel's Lotto Belisol. Voigt is captured honourably with 3km remaining and then it's flat out to the line.

There is the usual battling for pole position, universally presumed to be Cavendish's wheel. The World Champion is glued to his last lead-out man, Edvald Boasson Hagen, the Norwegian having blossomed into the role over the course of this race. What they really need is somebody blessed with a world-class pursuiter or time triallist's talent to tow them into the final few hundred metres. Where on earth would they find somebody like that?

In 1993, when Brad, Ryan and their mum were here as spectators, it was to see their hero Miguel Indurain win his third straight Tour. They craned their necks to see the big man in the yellow jersey buried deep in the heart of the bunch, safe in the knowledge that his race was won and he could relax in the bosom of his comrades until the final podium presentation later that afternoon.

The people who've journeyed across, over or under *la Manche* to see their own hero nineteen years later are luckier. They not only get to see the first British winner of the Tour de France, they get to see him lead the whole race under the final *flamme rouge* of the 2012 race. Wiggins is at full gas, the entire race struggling to hold the wheel of the yellow jersey, riding a newly liveried yellow Pinarello just for the occasion. When he pulls over as the peloton approaches the final elbow, Boasson Hagen takes up his pace and the Manx Missile readies himself. With a breathtaking blast of pure human muscle power Mark Cavendish hits the front *waaaaay* before anybody else would dream of doing. His initial rush is so great that it opens up a huge gap over Goss and Sagan. The game is up before there are even 200m left to go.

Of all the myriad eulogies and tributes that will pour in for the various achievements we have witnessed today, few will strike a more ringing chord than US star Taylor Phinney's tweet: 'Well, that was one of the coolest things I have ever seen.'

Team Sky have taken first and second place in the Tour de France. They have also won six stages. They are entitled to party. Amongst the clamouring hordes around his feet, Bradley Wiggins climbs on to the roof of a team car to accept the adulation.

On the podium, he is more sombre. Despite being a trailblazer, there is none of the bluster of the young Armstrong about Wiggins. He has lived and breathed cycling since he was a boy, watched others go through this magical ritual dozens of times since then. The profundity of the Champs-Élysées podium ceremony is not lost on him. The completeness of his victory has been clear for a few days now – only two men have finished within ten minutes of him and one of them is his teammate – and he has had time to consider the weight of this moment. Unlike a dazed footballer who finds himself with the FA Cup above his head minutes after a late winning goal at Wembley, Brad has coasted into Paris with the praise of the race, the press and the world ringing in his ears and resounding in his head.

The sportswriter Richard Williams dismisses the inevitable comparisons with Great British greats like Fred Perry and

Bobby Moore, instead alighting on a more suitable match in Mike Hawthorne. When he became the UK's first motor racing World Champion in 1958, Hawthorne broke a long tradition of Italians, Argentinians and French winners, opening the door for the proud list of British winners that have followed. Perhaps, muses Williams, that will be Wiggins's true legacy.

His humour, his humility, his honesty, his confidence and his talent have made Brad a popular winner of this race, despite France's natural antipathy for *les rosbifs*. A great cartoon in *L'Équipe* shows the yellow jersey's aquiline profile and sizeable sideburn, with the face furniture neatly shaped into a map of France.

Finally, the presentations complete, the obligatory shots of the winner looking wistfully over to the Arc de Triomphe in the can, Wiggins moves towards his public to say a few words. He has been planning these lines for some time, certainly the last few days, possibly the last couple of years, or even his whole life. He takes a deep breath and a hush falls as the gathered masses wait to hear exactly what it all means to this remarkable young man.

'Right,' he begins, 'we're going to draw the numbers for the raffle now.'

EPILOGUE:

Hampton Court
Wednesday, 1 August 2012

There aren't many people who've been to more bike races than Graham Watson. The world's best known cycling photographer covered his first Tour de France in 1977 and has been on the road pretty much uninterrupted since then. With his trusty companion and motorcycle pilot, former *Cycle Sport* editor Luke Evans, he sits enjoying what is probably his ten millionth pre-race coffee in a café near the start of a bike race.

But today is slightly different. For the first time in that long illustrious history of capturing bike races, Graham could have walked to the start from his front door. It's not even a long walk; it's the sort of walk you might take for a pint of milk or the Sunday papers. Because today the world is coming to Graham's front door. This is Hampton Court, this is London 2012, and this is the Olympic Time Trial. Even cycling photography's most impassive proponent is excited. Not excited like you or me, you understand, but excited. A little bit.

Graham has been photographing Bradley Wiggins since the late 1990s, but never more so than in 2012, and that's not a record that's about to end today.

Outside Henry VIII's front door, another Olympian is rubbing the sweat off his palms. Former GB Road Champion Matt Stephens was a competitor at Barcelona twenty years ago. Today his crucial Olympic role is to push off the riders as they sail down the start ramp to begin the 44km that separates them from golden glory.

Spain's time trial specialist Luis Leon Sanchez barely makes it off the ramp. A broken chain means his day is dead before it's begun. Oh, and Sanchez will get a puncture before his ride is over, too. Just how many black cats did he run over on his way here?

Brad is sandwiched between his twin nemeses. World Champion Tony Martin precedes him, and breathing down his neck in the start house is the reigning Olympic Champion Fabian Cancellara.

If there has ever been a crowd like this at a time trial before, it went unrecorded. Every yard of the course is covered with spectators. They were lining the barriers at 8.30 this morning, with Wiggins not scheduled to start until 3.07 p.m. Over six hours of waiting in the sun in stick-on ginger sideburns, peering at the world through the eyeholes in their Wiggins masks, handily supplied in this morning's tabloids for instant use. It's not an unknowledgeable crowd either. Armed with start sheets, a murmur goes along the barriers as the *cognoscenti* discuss the next rider as he approaches. Along Hampton Court Way, 10km in, the iPhone timers are out in force, calculations based on the 90-second gap between riders constantly whirring. Who's winning? The seeding is working out well enough for the answer to usually be: the next guy.

A rumble of anticipation sweeps up the road about ten seconds in advance of each competitor. When Jack Bauer of New Zealand flies around the corner that brings him into view a gasp precedes him as his fine margins nearly take him straight into the barriers.

Any notion that this is an ill-informed mob is lost when Vinokourov pounds past. The freshly crowned Olympic Road Champion's mixed history is obviously well known to this audience and he travels through to the sound of muted applause and scattered boos in stark contrast to the enthusiastic welcome afforded to everybody else so far.

A massive roar from the direction of the River Thames tells us that Chris Froome is on his way. The British love to adopt a winner. It's even better if he becomes a winner after they've adopted him, so Chris Froome is greeted like the homecoming hero he is. One of only two British riders in history to step on to the final GC podium in Paris, it's probably reasonable to expect his reception will be eclipsed by the other one when he arrives in a few minutes' time, but it's hard to imagine this lot getting any more excited than they are at seeing the Kenyan-born climber in the flesh. He sails through on a tide of noise, the fastest so far.

Tony Martin is on his way now. The cycling fans hold their breath as they await the German, knowing a true challenger to their man has arrived. The other spectators chuckle to themselves, remembering that Tony Martin was the name of the Norfolk farmer who took a shotgun to a pair of burglars and found himself a *cause célèbre* a few years ago. Martin is certainly giving it both barrels and comes through the corridor of noise like the proverbial speeding bullet. Fastest.

In some ways, there could be no more pressure on Brad. Those not familiar with the tangled intricacies of road racing were left entirely bemused by Mark Cavendish's failure to top the charts on The Mall at the weekend. 'Seven years he had to prepare for that and he comes nowhere,' was not a unique reaction amongst armchair sports fans over their newspapers on Sunday morning. Scandalously, that view was even shared by some ill-informed hacks filling their pages. Cav's adoption by the Great British public to become BBC Sports Personality of the Year is not enough alone to earn him exemption from national expectancy. Now that weight has passed to the skinny shoulders of Wiggins. These Games are now into their fifth day and this city is baying for British gold.

On the other hand, what the hell? This *annus mirabilis* is in the bag. Paris–Nice led to the Tour de Romandie and on to the Dauphiné and up to the Tour de France with scarcely a misplaced turn of the pedals among them. Unbeaten in long time trials despite Martin and Cancellara's best efforts, who cares about a little local affair that carries more weight with the great unwashed than the true devotees who travelled to the Champs-Elysées to celebrate the arrival of Golden Sideburns the weekend before last?

Here comes the answer. The red aero helmet is perfectly still, the spine of the GB skinsuit entirely flat, the pedal stroke impeccably even, the speed perceptibly fast. Powered by noise, the sound of his carbon disc wheel drowned out by a thousand hollering Wiggo-lovers, he heads to the first time check and a narrow lead over Martin.

Only Spartacus remains. The great man has passed himself fit after inexplicably flying head first into the barriers outside the Star and Garter home for military veterans in Richmond Park during Saturday's road race. Destined to be known by thousands of southwest London cyclists as Cancellara Corner forever more, the deceptively innocuous curve had caused a miscalculation in the defending Olympic TT Champion as he looked behind to discover the whereabouts of the chasing bunch at exactly the wrong moment. Right arm dangling loosely at his side after a hefty thwack on the shoulder, he ploughed on to the finish in central London, when a quick pedal back to the Swiss hotel at Hampton Court might have been a better plan. X-rays showed no structural damage, but deep bruising and intense discomfort put his participation in the time trial in serious doubt. Would he be able to hold his aero position for 44km? Would he lose some of his legendary power? With Wiggins in the form of his life and a sound beating of the Swiss icon in the bag at Besançon just a couple of weeks ago, surely Cancellara would need to be at 100% to retain his crown.

Frankly, despite the welcome from a crowd delighted to see the world's most popular cyclist on their own turf, it's clear that this is unlikely to be Cancellara's day. Rocking slightly as he tries to find some comfort, it's clear that he's not going to be able to stay within the 90 seconds of Wiggins that he needs to get on the podium.

The Tour de France Champion, three times an Olympic Champion, Bradley Wiggins OBE, unbeaten in long time trials in 2012, on home roads. He's not going to lose today, is he?

★

The Prince of Wales public house is within about 100m of Hampton Court Bridge, separated from the palace itself by the grey water of the Thames. They do a decent trade on summer weekends and have a lively local clientele on Friday and Saturday evenings all year round. Their busiest time in the hundred years since the doors first opened, however, is around 3.30 p.m. on Wednesday, 1 August 2012. Several hundred people are crammed into the high-ceilinged main bar where a selection of big-screen TVs are all tuned to the Olympic event unfolding outside. There are a couple of hundred more in the street outside, pressed to the windows to catch a glimpse of one of the screens. Chinese whispers run through the crowd.

'What's happening?'

'Brad's coming up to the first time check.'

'No, that's Froome.'

'Oh, OK.'

'That's actually the second time check.'

'Oh. Come on, Wiggo!'

Nobody needs reminding of the sporting rivalry between Britain and Germany. Rumours abound of Bob Paisley gathering his Liverpool players before the European Cup Final against Borussia Mönchengladbach to tell them, 'These blokes' dads were shooting at your dads 30 years ago.' Multiple international football disasters for England at the hands of the Germans have not helped home fans, as they cling to the distant memory of their solitary World Cup win in 1966. The Prince of Wales has quite an atmosphere as alongside the Team GB supporters, there are 30 or so noisy Germans cheering for Tony Martin.

It's not a poisonous atmosphere, but it's loud, passionate and with an edge, especially when an enormous black, red and yellow Bundesflagge is unfurled and waved maniacally, blocking the view of the TV. 'There's only *ooooooone* Bradley Wiggins,' to the tune of 'Walking In A Winter Wonderland' breaks out through the pub and on to the street. The crowd is swelling by the minute as spectators heading from the route to the finish realise they're not going to be able to see anything at

Hampton Court. The singing begins to resonate down the narrow road as the excitement and tension grows.

Martin soars through the second check with the quickest time so far, reawakening the German fans temporarily drowned out by the singing. A minute or so follows with the tension rising as we await the arrival of Wiggins. A hush begins to fall. The press of the crowd grows as everybody squints at the tiny clock in the bottom corner of the screen. Here he comes. Click. -22 seconds. Hysteria breaks out. No penalty kick hitting the back of a German net was ever greeted with more euphoria.

He's going to do it.

On the TV, Hugh Porter is watching Tony Martin close in on Taylor Phinney as they hammer down the long drive that leads through Bushy Park to the palace. But his colleague Chris Boardman, bronze medallist in this event in Atlanta in 1996, has noticed a more pertinent fact: Wiggins has entered the park and has both of them in his sights. Only a disaster can stop him now.

The 2012 Bradley Wiggins doesn't do disasters.

As he hits the line, the roar in the Prince of Wales is matched in the street, across the bridge at Hampton Court, across the host city of London, across the nation. Great Britain is singing. Walking along, singing a song, walking in a Wiggo wonderland. We all need heroes, and this summer has given Britain a new favourite.

Palmarès

1998
1st, Individual Pursuit, Junior World Track Championships, Havana
2nd, Team Pursuit, Commonwealth Games, Kuala Lumpur

2000
2nd, Team Pursuit, World Track Championships, Manchester
3rd, Team Pursuit, Olympic Games, Sydney

2002
2nd, Individual Pursuit, Commonwealth Games, Manchester
2nd, Team Pursuit, Commonwealth Games, Manchester
2nd, Ghent Six Day

2003
1st, Individual Pursuit, World Track Championships, Stuttgart
2nd, Team Pursuit, World Track Championships, Stuttgart

2004
1st, Individual Pursuit, Olympic Games, Athens
2nd, Team Pursuit, Olympic Games, Athens
3rd, Madison, Olympic Games, Athens

2005
1st, Stage 8, Tour de l'Avenir

2007

1st, Individual Pursuit, World Track Championships, Mallorca
1st, Team Pursuit, World Track Championships, Mallorca
1st, Stage 1, Four Days of Dunkirk
1st, Stage 4, Tour du Poitou-Charentes et de la Vienne
1st, Prologue, Critérium du Dauphiné
1st, Duo Normand
Combativity Award, Stage 6, Tour de France

2008

1st, Individual Pursuit, World Track Championships, Manchester
1st, Team Pursuit, World Track Championships, Manchester
1st, Madison, World Track Championships, Manchester
1st, Individual Pursuit, Olympic Games, Beijing
1st, Team Pursuit, Olympic Games, Beijing

2009

1st, Stage 1, Tour of Qatar
1st, Stage 3b, Three Days of De Panne
1st, National Time Trial Championships
1st, Stage 5, Herald Sun Tour
1st, Overall, Herald Sun Tour
4th, Overall, Tour de France

2010

1st, Stage 1, Tour of Qatar
1st, Stage 1, Giro d'Italia
1st, National Time Trial Championships

2011

1st, Stage 4, Bayern Rundfahrt
1st, Overall, Critérium du Dauphiné
1st, National Road Race Championships
2nd, Time Trial, World Road Championships

3rd, Overall, Paris–Nice
3rd, Overall, Vuelta a España

2012
1st, Stage 5, Volta ao Algarve
3rd, Overall, Volta ao Algarve
1st, Stage 8, Paris–Nice
1st, Overall, Paris–Nice
1st, Stage 1, Tour de Romandie
1st, Stage 5, Tour de Romandie
1st, Overall, Tour de Romandie
1st, Stage 4, Critérium du Dauphiné
1st, Overall, Critérium du Dauphiné
1st, Stage 9, Tour de France
1st, Stage 19, Tour de France
1st, Overall, Tour de France
1st, Time Trial, Olympic Games, London

Afterword

Paul McCartney had to wait until he was 54. Mick Jagger was 60. Winston Churchill was an MP at 25, but he had to get to the ripe old age of 78 to get his.

In December 2012 Great Britain recognised the impact of Bradley Wiggins's incredible sporting feats by handing him a knighthood at the remarkably young age of 32. Already a CBE thanks to his earlier Herculean Olympic efforts, the powers that be clearly felt there was nowhere else he should go but right up to the top of the honours tree. The New Year's honours list proclaimed our hero a Knight Bachelor. Arise, Sir Bradley. And while we're at it, arise Sir Dave Brailsford, 30 years younger than Churchill when Her Madge laid the sword on their respective shoulders. Mystifyingly to his legions of fans, the directeur sportif who guided Brad to his achievements in 2012 still remains Mr S. Yates with no letters after his name despite his many personal triumphs, but now is not the time to quibble. Now is the time to bask in the reflective glory of a golden year.

And never mind the powers that be, what about the man in the street? The man on the Clapham omnibus? Well, he seems to agree with that lot upstairs, as he voted Brad BBC Sports Personality of the Year 2012. Now, there has been a groundswell of interest in cycling in recent years, with both Sir Chris Hoy (also knighted at 32, good effort) and Mark Cavendish MBE scooping the title, but 2012 was a golden year for British sporting achievement. Lest we forget, this was the year that Andy Murray won the US Open, Rory McIlroy became world number one and won the US PGA by eight shots, Ian Poulter inspired Europe to the greatest turnaround in Ryder Cup history, Alastair Cook became the scorer of more England centuries than anybody else ever, and Chelsea won the European Cup . . . And we haven't even mentioned the Olympics.

Poor Mo Farah must curse the moment that Bradley crashed out of the 2011 Tour. 'Why couldn't he have won it last year?' he must have whispered to his wife at the star-studded ceremony at ExCel. In how many other years would the British winner of a 5,000 and 10,000 metres Olympic double miss out on the SPOTY award?

In sport, career retrospectives are usually reserved until retirement. In team sport, it often doesn't even happen then: a player retires, but the team rolls on from one generation to another, always looking forward. It is against this uniquely challenging backdrop of acclaim and applause that Brad has to attempt to remain at the pinnacle of his sport. Preparation for 2013 must have been exceedingly difficult in the circumstances, despite having the experience of his post-Athens 2004 bender under his belt.

And who would begrudge Bradley his fun? Turning up on stage with a cherry red Gibson 335 to play alongside Paul Weller at Hammersmith Odeon at Christmas, knocking out the Modfather's classic 'That's Entertainment'. This was still his moment, and the 2013 season seemed a long way off.

Brad revealed in an interview with Alasdair Fotheringham about his taste in music for *Cycle Sport* – expect race reports from the Giro d'Italia in the *NME* this year – that his true musical hero is actually John Entwistle, The Who's late bass player. The tall, skinny, reserved cool-guy look is certainly much more Entwistle than Weller, and so are the sideburns. Weller's never really been one for the big boards; he grows his hair long and combs it in front of his ears, another Bradley style favourite, but John Entwistle wore luxuriant face furniture to inspire a generation.

The fascinating Sky dichotomy between Brad and Chris

Froome is yet to play out. With the 2013 Tour de France set to be more mountainous than the defending champion would like, Brad threw his weight behind the notion that he would concentrate his personal efforts on gaining a Giro d'Italia pink winner's jersey to go with his French yellow, before going to the Tour as Froome's helper. Within weeks of that Sky-sponsored point of view, Sir Bradley was mischievously suggesting to the *Guardian* that he would 'love to win a second Tour de France'.

Chris Froome opened 2013 in surprisingly strong form for one who is not expected to be at his peak until July. His storming performance to take February's Tour of Oman was, astonishingly, his first stage race victory, and came at the expense of renowned mountain experts like Joaquim Rodríguez and Alberto Contador. Bradley, in contrast, finished last on the first stage of Oman, having been caught up in a crash, but recovered to end the week in the middle of the pack.

Froome went on to Italy and took the lead in a superbly hard-fought Tirreno–Adriatico, but was forced out of the winner's jersey by his Tour de France rival Vincenzo Nibali. Their Sky teammates were preparing for spring at the now tried-and-trusted training camp, hoping once again to get the jump on their rivals once the real racing began. Nibali versus Wiggins is the sub-text for the 2013 Giro d'Italia. Bradley's defence of – or decision not to defend – the Tour de France that follows on the heels of that Giro will be shaped by events in Italy.

In 1985, the last truly great French cyclist Bernard Hinault won his fifth Tour de France, benefiting in no small way from the assistance of a dazzlingly talented young American teammate, Greg LeMond. 'The Badger' paid tribute to LeMond by saying that he would be at his side to help him take his own victory the next year. When 1986 came round, the temptation of becoming a record-breaking six-time Tour winner proved too much for Hinault, and he attacked his bewildered lieutenant-cum-leader through the Pyrénées, shaping one of the greatest ever Tours. The duo eventually finished first and second, begging the question: was that really so bad for the team?

An unprecedented successive one-two in Paris in 2013 may well be a Sky dream scenario, and one not beyond the realms of possibility. The identity of the man on the top step, however, can only remain a matter for speculation.

One thing is certain; the giddy car-top Champs-Élysées celebrations of July 2012 will never be repeated in quite the same manner. Only once can a man say: today I became the first ever British winner of the Tour de France.

Acknowledgements

My sincere thanks to all those who accommodated my key-tapping: Dr Weiss, The Blue Groove, The Rock, The Manor, Crumbs Too, Marine Girl, and, of course, Mum and Dad. Thank you Buddy and Daisy for constant inspiration. Thank you Kt, Knobby, Gary and Mungo for wisely standing by me. And thank you Bob, E, Geddy, Alex and Neil for keeping me awake.

John Deering